The Refusalist International

Theory Redux series
Series editor: Laurent de Sutter

Published Titles
Mark Alizart, *Cryptocommunism*
Armen Avanessian, *Future Metaphysics*
Franco Berardi, *The Second Coming*
Alfie Bown, *The Playstation Dreamworld*
Alfie Bown, *Post-Comedy*
Laurent de Sutter, *Narcocapitalism*
Diedrich Diederichsen, *Aesthetics of Pop Music*
Mladen Dolar, *Rumors*
Roberto Esposito, *Persons and Things*
Boris Groys, *Becoming an Artwork*
Graham Harman, *Immaterialism*
Helen Hester, *Xenofeminism*
Srećko Horvat, *The Radicality of Love*
Lorenzo Marsili, *Planetary Politics*
Fabian Muniesa, *Paranoid Finance*
Dominic Pettman, *Infinite Distraction*
Eloy Fernández Porta, *Nomography*
Andreas Philippopoulos-Mihalopoulos, *Hydrojustice*
Mikkel Bolt Rasmussen, *Late Capitalist Fascism*
Mikkel Bolt Rasmussen, *The Refusalist International*
Gerald Raunig, *Making Multiplicity*
Helen Rollins, *Psychocinema*
Avital Ronell, *America*
Nick Srnicek, *Platform Capitalism*
Grafton Tanner, *Foreverism*
Oxana Timofeeva, *Solar Politics*
Alenka Zupančič, *Disavowal*

The Refusalist International

A Theory of the New Protest Cycle

Mikkel Bolt Rasmussen

polity

Copyright © Mikkel Bolt Rasmussen 2025

The right of Mikkel Bolt Rasmussen to be identified as Author of this Work has been asserted in accordance with the UK Copyright, Designs and Patents Act 1988.

First published in 2025 by Polity Press Ltd.

Polity Press Ltd.
65 Bridge Street
Cambridge CB2 1UR, UK

Polity Press Ltd.
111 River Street
Hoboken, NJ 07030, USA

All rights reserved. Except for the quotation of short passages for the purpose of criticism and review, no part of this publication may be reproduced, stored in a retrieval system or transmitted, in any form or by any means, electronic, mechanical, photocopying, recording or otherwise, without the prior permission of the publisher.

ISBN-13: 978-1-5095-6827-7
ISBN-13: 978-1-5095-6828-4 (pb)

A catalogue record for this book is available from the British Library.

Library of Congress Control Number: 2025935952

Typeset in 12.5 on 15pt Adobe Garamond
by Cheshire Typesetting Ltd, Cuddington, Cheshire
Printed and bound in Great Britain by Ashford Colour Ltd

The publisher has used its best endeavours to ensure that the URLs for external websites referred to in this book are correct and active at the time of going to press. However, the publisher has no responsibility for the websites and can make no guarantee that a site will remain live or that the content is or will remain appropriate.

Every effort has been made to trace all copyright holders, but if any have been overlooked the publisher will be pleased to include any necessary credits in any subsequent reprint or edition.

For further information on Polity, visit our website:
politybooks.com

How do I do it and where do I start?
Surely everyone knows this better for oneself
than anybody else ever could: no more
leaders, no more teachers, no more students,
here comes the time of inventing new
mediations between people.
Claire Fontaine[1]

Find the self, then kill it.
Amiri Baraka[2]

Contents

Acknowledgements		ix
1	Introduction	1
2	The Globalization of Protest	15
3	The New Movement	31
4	Refusal	42
5	Aphasia	48
6	The End of Reformism	53
7	Anti-Politics	60
8	The Workers' Movement	66
9	The Socialist Horizon and Beyond	78
10	Dissolution	88
11	Refusal of the Refusal	94
Notes		107

Acknowledgements

Numerous people and groups have helped bring this book into being, too many to name, but special thanks to Kieran Aarons, Joshua Clover, Carsten Juhl, Dominique Routhier, Katarina Stenbeck, the group at Fredag Aften, the Ill Will cohorts, as well as the team at Polity, most notably Manuela Tecusan, John Thompson and Lindsey Wimpenny.

I

Introduction

The stakes were high. Late capitalist society's powers of absorption seemed only to grow. Everything appeared as if the working class, still toiling in the centres of accumulation, had finally been integrated through consumerism, a rising standard of living and the culture industry.

The publication of *One-Dimensional Man* in 1964 found Herbert Marcuse at his most pessimistic: advanced industrial society, he claimed, was the culmination of a historical dynamic in which the oppression of humankind increased in lockstep with its technological development, which in principle could have liberated it, but did not. The atom bomb, which presented the threat of total annihilation, was emblematic of this situation. At the same time the new society exerted an almost complete ideological control over human subjectivity, and in consequence effectively integrated the proletariat.

Marcuse gazed out upon a society that appeared to transcend the contradictions of capitalist economy. One-dimensional society was industrially advanced; it had soaring productivity and a staggering growth rate that enabled the material improvement of the lives of most people (at least in the West). It signalled a metamorphosis of capitalism in which living standards might continuously improve for the middle and working classes, which no longer had any reason to oppose the system. An ever-increasing tide of goods enabled people's smooth integration into a classless class society.

But this new society was still a capitalist society characterized by unsolvable contradictions. The changes were merely quantitative: human beings had exchanged the possibility of a free, self-determined future for high living standards and access to cheap commodities. Yet if the working class was no longer the obvious, or even the plausible spearhead of a socialist revolution, it was not easy to identify a lever that could transcend capitalist society. Marcuse could no longer muster belief in the proletariat. As he put it, 'dialectical theory is not refuted, but it cannot offer the remedy'.[1]

It was not easy. Marcuse was a Marxist philosopher. He was living in the United States, where he had accepted a professorship in philosophy at Brandeis in Massachusetts, and was now in his mid-sixties. As a young man he had taken part in the German Revolution of 1918–19 as member of a soldiers' council in Berlin, having been enthused by the words and deeds of Rosa Luxemburg and the other Spartacists. The revolution was brutally crushed by the combined forces of the German Social Democratic Party and proto-fascist Freikorps troops, an experience that left a lasting impression on the young Marcuse. The necessity of a total historical rupture with the money economy and the state form would remain a constant feature of his thinking: there was no place for any social democratic compromise, he had seen first-hand the consequences of that in 1919 – including the murders of Luxemburg and Karl Liebknecht. After studies with Husserl and Heidegger in Freiburg in the late 1920s, Marcuse was forced to leave Germany in 1933 and ended up in the United States. There he participated in the exiled Marxist 'think tank' that was the Frankfurt School before becoming a professor at Brandeis.

One-Dimensional Man may be read as Marcuse's attempt to keep the dream of the German Revolution alive. This would prove to be an uphill battle. Everything looked as if the money economy in Western Europe and North America had found a way to supersede its internal crisis tendencies. By the late 1950s and early 1960s, when Marcuse wrote the book, what we now call *les trente glorieuses* (the Glorious Thirty) felt as if those years (1945–75) could last forever. The post-war economic boom enabled the ruling classes in the West to leverage welfare and culture as tools for a bloodless pacification of the toiling masses. The capital–labour relation not merely was consolidated but appeared set in stone.

Marcuse's analysis in *One-Dimensional Man* is bleak. The possibilities for radical social transformation appear to be voided. However, towards the end of the book, he nevertheless gestures towards the possibility of radical critique, or what he calls 'a radical refusal':[2] insofar as people can refuse, 'denying the positive', they can still break free from existing society and emancipate themselves.³ Once human nature has been absorbed into the system of capitalist commodity production, the only alternative lies in a wholesale refusal. If one-dimensional society constitutes the materialization of ideology, its negation would need to be 'the pure form of negation'.⁴ The only possible opposition, therefore, lies in an abstract refusal, a total negation of the existing order:

> All content seems reduced to the one abstract demand for the end of domination – the only truly revolutionary exigency, and the event that would validate the achievements of industrial civilization. In the face of its efficient denial by the established system, this negation appears in the politically impotent form of 'the absolute refusal' – a refusal which seems all the more unreasonable the more the established system develops its productivity and alleviates the burden of life.⁵

The dialectical movement of history has broken down. The gravediggers of capitalism, the proletariat, have been transformed into consumers. But it is still possible to refuse. The refusal of marginal groups in bourgeois society might still trigger a revolutionary process whereby the working classes in the advanced industrial countries could become *Klasse für sich* (class for itself), that is, become the revolutionary subject.

The cards were stacked against Marcuse. The more the worker became integrated into class society, the more unreasonable radical critique seemed to be. Why contest affluent society, if it was ameliorating everybody's lives in the West, if workers had access to jobs, housing, education and culture – in other words, if they could share in the affluence of industrially advanced societies? Part of the challenge here concerns the integration of the superstructure into the productive sphere, thanks to the increasing entanglement of culture and economy. The consumer economy, Marcuse writes, creates 'a second nature [for] man', libidinally lashing human beings to the commodity form. One-dimensional humans voluntarily subject themselves to the demands of consumption. The revolution therefore necessitates the development of new desires, 'which might precondition man for freedom'.[6] The struggle for a new society would be the struggle for new passions.

Marcuse refers here to the French author and literary critic Maurice Blanchot, who had written about the need for refusal in a short text published in 1958, at the height of the Algerian Revolution. Marcuse highlights the abstract and total character of Blanchot's refusal: it is necessary to refuse without grounds, Blanchot insists. Marcuse, however, interprets the claim slightly differently, situating it in a Marxist framework: if the refusal was abstract, this was because it signalled a rejection of reification. If Blanchot's refusal amounted to an evacuation or a refusal of politics (which, for Blanchot, coincided with de Gaulle's assumption of power), Marcuse's was a historically specific refusal of the consumer economy, of the integrated society of advanced capitalism. One-dimensional society was a society without opposition: this was the challenge Marcuse sought to face up to. There were still classes, of course – the bourgeoisie and the working class – but they were no longer agents of historical transformation. Both materially and ideologically, the working class had been integrated into the capitalist system, which effectively debunked the Marxian concept of revolution. Capitalism seemed to have found a way of escaping the perils of class structure; the proletariat was nowhere to be seen. Its integration into the capitalist system was achieved not merely through the dynamism of the production process itself but also because it shared the needs of capitalism. The historical subject that could bring an end to capitalist exploitation – and, with this, to prehistory more generally – was lacking. In such a situation, the idea of a blanket refusal provided Marcuse with a much needed internal–external opposition to the 'affluent' one-dimensional society.

In conditions of almost unprecedented prosperity, the revolutionary perspective assumed the form of a radical refusal of the new life proffered by the consumer society. For Marcuse, emerging subcultures such as those of the hippies were an example of people 'refusing to play the game'.[7] These were small groups that had broken with the familiar. They were rejecting routine ways of doing things, experimenting with new modes of living, creating new forms of political affect.

Whereas previous historical forms of critique could count on forces within capitalist society to bring society down from within, this was no longer the case. As Marcuse put it, '[t]he struggle for the solution has outgrown the traditional forms [of revolution]. The totalitarian tendencies of the one-dimensional society render the traditional ways and means of protest ineffective.'[8] It was necessary to look beyond the forms of established working-class opposition and Marxist theory. This led Marcuse to the only remaining proto-revolutionary forces, namely those excluded from affluence: the non-integrated 'outsiders'. 'Underneath the conservative popular base is the substratum of the outcast and outsiders, the exploited and persecuted of other races and other colours, the unemployed and the unemployable.'[9] In other words, the beginning of the end lay in the hands of the most exploited, whose 'opposition hits the system from without', Marcuse wrote.[10] The proletariat, the conscious agents of historical change, had been replaced by those who had been cast aside, the most persecuted outsiders. Such groups might not be class-conscious, but they nonetheless refuse the one-dimensional society. Their 'opposition' was 'revolutionary, even if their consciousness [was] not'.[11] They constituted a militant minority – a *détonateur* (trigger), as Marcuse would put it in French in a later text.[12]

In retrospect, Marcuse's analysis of the integration of the working class in the West and the emergence of new rebellious subjects proved to be spot-on. In the late 1960s, dissatisfaction with the consumer society grew exponentially and students, young people, migrant workers and groups on the fringes of the economy began to protest against the post-war compromise. May '68 is often used as a shorthand to refer to the broad global protest culture that swept the world for several years and, in places like Italy, would last until 1977.

Why return today to Marcuse's writings of the mid-1960s? The point is certainly not to emphasize the similarities between his era and ours, the way in which the capitalist economy reinvents itself so as to take on new old forms of accumulation, exploitation, exclusion and control. Marcuse was living in an age of soaring productivity rates quite unlike what we see in today's global economy, which has been in tatters for decades. The point, as I see it, is to underscore instead Marcuse's effort to affirm a different way of opposing political and economic power. He tried to describe a different mode of anti-capitalist struggle. What is more, he was partly right: new revolutionary subjects did emerge onto the scene during the 1960s, even if May '68 still took place largely under the banner of Marxist class struggle. For the revolutionaries of this decade, the question was still one of taking power and socializing production. Even in Bologna in 1977, when we see the culmination of the protests of the previous decade, most groups still subscribed to an idea of society in class struggle. It is this notion of society – in class struggle – that has disappeared today. Now we have protests – an enormous number of them, in fact – but the vision of a different society is nowhere to be found. That vision seems to have evaporated.

In current-day struggles we still find people engaging in refusal, yet they are doing so without possessing any vision of a different society. Those who revolt today do not do so in the service of ideas, laid out in advance, about a different economy or about other groups or classes that may run the current economy or head up the state apparatus. This book is an attempt to understand these seemingly blank protests wherein people refuse the existing order without proposing an alternative. I shall argue that the protests that have taken place across the globe since 2011 do indeed constitute a movement: a *movement of refusal*, which experiments with new kinds of political action beyond the usual frameworks of sovereignty and representation.

The slogan 'The people want the fall of the regime', which was launched during the Arab revolts of 2010 and 2011, has become an emblem of these mass protests, which have moved discontinuously across the globe over the past fifteen years. Most of the demonstrations, riots and occupations that have taken place the world over – from North Africa to Southern Europe, from Chile to Hong Kong via Turkey and France, from Bangladesh to Iran – have opposed local governments: 'The people want the fall of the regime.' It is as if an unbridgeable abyss had opened between governments and populations in countries across the world. 'The people' are refusing to be governed by their rulers: whether these be democratically elected politicians or dictators, they all must go.

What I call 'the movement of refusal' – or, even more high-key, 'the Refusalist International' – has obviously been a feature of most previous historical struggles against capitalist social relations and their enforcement through state mediation, but during the past few decades it has begun to come into its own as a particular form of oppositional practice. This book is an attempt to describe this movement and its emergence.

In the early 1960s Marcuse had a hunch that something was changing, that a previous revolutionary practice and the specific revolutionary vocabulary that sustained it were beginning to break down. Well aware of the obsolescence of the dominant language of revolution in the nineteenth and twentieth century, he points us in the direction of a new one. He, of course, never got to see it – and perhaps would not have recognized it anyway. Today's movement is very different from those he knew and hoped to advance.

In retrospect, it is evident that May '68, the upheaval Marcuse helped to bring into being analytically, signalled a partial rediscovery of the proletarian revolutionary offensive of 1917–21. The new cycle of protest that began in earnest in 2011 is, for better or worse, an entirely new beginning. The mass protests that have unfolded at an uneven staccato virtually everywhere in the world over the past thirteen to fourteen years no longer make any reference to the workers' movement's models of social transformation, whether social democratic, Leninist, Eurocommunist, or council communist. The *indiani metropolitani* (metropolitan Indians) of the 1977 movement in Italy still made fun of Marxism and the revolutionary tradition, tagging 'After Marx, April' and 'After Mao, June' on the walls of Bologna. No one does that anymore. The new protests are taking place in a political vacuum. This explains their characteristic of being at once strangely loud and violent, but also silent. It's as if the protesters were totally silent when they took to the streets, demanding that this or that reform be rolled back, or demanding this or that politician out of the presidential palace or parliament. The new mass protests are refusing everyone and everything. And they are doing so without any reference to pre-established dogmas, agreements or principles. This is what we need to understand.

2

The Globalization of Protest

There have been so many mass protests around the world in the past fifteen years that attempting to name even the most important ones leaves one breathless: the Arab Spring revolts that erupted in 2010–2011; the Southern European Movement of the Squares in 2011 and the Occupy Wall Street that same year; the Maidan Uprising in Ukraine, the pro-democracy protests in Hong Kong and the Ferguson riots in the United States, all in 2014; the Yellow Vests in France in 2018; the violent riots in Chile and the Lebanese uprising, both in the next year; the feminist uprising in Iran in 2022; and the demonstrations and university encampments that took place worldwide in 2024 against the Israeli state's genocide in Gaza.

The recent period has undoubtedly been characterized by mass protests. And I didn't even mention the riots in London in 2011, the Brazilian transport revolt in 2013, or the Gezi Park protests in Istanbul that same year, the Sudanese revolution in 2019, the George Floyd revolt in 2020, more democracy protests in Hong Kong in 2019–2020, the feminist demonstrations in Argentina from 2015 to 2021, and the numerous climate activist movements, from Standing Rock and Ende Gelände (Here and No Further) to Les Soulèvements de la Terre (Earth Uprisings) and the Struggle to Defend the Atlanta Forest (also known as the Stop Cop City movement). On every continent, we have witnessed people taking to the streets protesting. A report published by the US think tank Center for Strategic and International Studies asserts that 'we are living in a time of global mass protests unprecedented in frequency, scope and scale'.[1] According to the report's authors, the number of protests increased by more than 11 per cent from 2009 to 2019 in all regions of the world. More and more people are rejecting what the Italian left-wing communist Giorgio Cesarano called 'the organic composition of late capitalism', in which survival is possible only through wage labour and money.² After five decades of declining growth in the world economy accompanied by the generalization of precarious and informal work everywhere, more and more people are taking to the streets. To say that capital is on its last legs is undoubtedly premature, but more and more people seem ready to protest against deteriorating living conditions, growing inequality, racial–colonial violence and an accelerating climate crisis.

If the period from the 1980s to the first decade of the new century was characterized by a striking absence of conflict and mass protests in the so-called First World and regular but rarely successful food riots and protests in the Second and Third World, we now live in a globalized world in which mass protests take place everywhere. These protests take the form of demonstrations, occupations or riots, and over the past fifteen years have on several occasions developed into full-blown uprisings or revolts, for example in North Africa and the Middle East in 2011, in Ukraine in 2014, and in Sudan in 2019. As Dilip Gaonkar writes, the protests in the Global South have not only grown in strength but have also moved northwards.³ It is as if there had been a generalization of misery, depression, climate anxiety and poverty, such that young people in both the South and the North stare despairingly into a disintegrating world. That's why so many of them are taking to the streets. Vulnerability and agency have become intertwined, just as Judith Butler writes – but without affording any new programme.[4]

It can be difficult to get a picture of the protests and their scope, both while they are unfolding and in retrospect. Like in wildfires, they suddenly flare up, die out, and then the fire explodes again somewhere else. As one can see from the various protest maps that the French anthropologist Alain Bertho and think tanks such as the Carnegie Endowment regularly produce, we are dealing with a discontinuous and unpredictable flow of events in which something is constantly happening, but with a lot of bad timing; one protest ends and another one breaks out somewhere else.[5]

Take the case of France, where demonstrations in March 2016 against a labour market reform developed into an occupation movement known as Nuit debout (Rise Up at Night). Protesters not only took over the Place de la République in Paris as well as squares in several other French cities, but also developed a new offensive tactic, called *cortège de tête* ('front bloc'), whereby a small group of protesters line up in front of the official part of a demonstration, with the deliberate aim of engaging the police. After nearly two months of protests, which ended in a large demonstration in front of the National Assembly as it was preparing to pass the law on the proposed labour reform, the Up all Night movement went back to sleep.

In November and December 2018, the Macron government's plan for a new fuel tax prompted thousands of people to don the yellow safety jackets (*gilets jaunes*) that drivers in France are required by law to carry in case of a car accident. Roundabouts, highways and toll booths were blocked all across France. Actions were not limited to traffic junctions in rural areas and small towns but also took place in large numbers in many major cities. President Macron was routinely burned or beheaded in effigy. In Paris they set fire to high-end restaurants, looted luxury shops and attacked the Arc de Triomphe on the Champs-Élysées. Although the catalyst for the movement was the proposed fuel surcharge, the protests quickly became about everything else too. In fact so many different demands were made that it soon became impossible for the government and local politicians to make sense of them. It didn't help that the movement, which had come together via social media, refused to nominate spokespersons or representatives. Whenever someone stood up and tried to take on such a role during demonstrations or in the media, they were swiftly shut down and shunned by others, and the protests would continue regardless.

The scale, unpredictability and ferocity of the protests and occupations were sufficiently overwhelming for Macron to feel compelled to withdraw the fuel tax. He also organized a large-scale and somewhat bizarre national debate, in which he travelled the country, attending debate meetings in order to present an image of a listening and caring politician, if nothing else. However, none of his initiatives succeeded in quelling the movement and the protests continued weekend after weekend for more than six months, in spite of shockingly callous repressive measures taken by the state. Police routinely fired teargas, flash-ball guns and rubber bullets directly into the faces of protesters, many of whom lost their eyes. Between November 2018 and February 2019 more than 2,000 protesters were injured. In March the government deployed the army after more than 100 luxury shops were looted on the Champs-Élysées. At the same time, the French Supreme Court rejected a proposal to ban police from using flash-ball guns. Later that month, a large group of lawyers published an open letter strongly criticizing the police's handling of the protests and questioning the slow procedure for dealing with complaints of police brutality when compared to the large number of quick convictions of protesters.

If we zoom out for a moment, it becomes clear that the Yellow Vests movement is in many ways exemplary of the many mass protests that have taken place over the past twelve to fifteen years. As the sociologist Michalis Lianos has described, the Yellow Vests was neither a revolt or revolution nor a social movement in the traditional sense.[6] None of the traditional political and sociological categories fits the profile of this phenomenon: there were no leaders, the participants were for the most part not politically active or members of parties or trade unions, and the occupation of roundabouts is not part of the regular repertoire of the French labour movement. Unions are not in the habit of gathering at roundabouts in small towns throughout the country and burning car tires. As Tristan Leoni writes, one of the surprising things about the Yellow Vests was 'that French workers felt compelled to use methods – wildcat demonstrations and riots – thought to be reserved for their counterparts in South America, Africa and Asia'.[7] The protests were thus unlike anything previously seen in France. Moreover, they were difficult to square with the classic distinction between right-wing and left-wing politics. These protests were different; and they just kept happening week after week. However, during the long hot summer of 2019 they finally seemed to die down.

Then, only a few months later, in December 2019, something happened again. The Macron government sought to implement pension reforms that would drastically limit the ability of a wide range of labour groups to retire – as previous governments had done in 2003, 2010 and 2013. When the plans were announced, they sparked not only huge local demonstrations in which up to 1 million people took part in Paris alone, but also nationwide strikes that paralysed train and air traffic for several weeks. A number of official as well as wildcat strikes took place across the country, and workers from a wide range of companies took direct action. Workers from electricity giant EDF, for example, cut power to Amazon's warehouses in France and to houses of politicians from Macron's party, while restoring it to a number of homeowners and homes that had been unable to pay their electricity bills.

The reforms were taken off the table in early 2020, before being relaunched in an expanded form in January 2023, when demonstrations and strikes were once again organized by the major trade unions, while some occurred spontaneously outside official institutions. What was most remarkable about the 2023 sequence of struggles was the extent to which it overflowed the traditional organizations, which lagged behind and scrambled to both understand and mediate the protests. As in the case of the Yellow Vests, the form taken by these new mass protests was altogether different from those seen throughout the twentieth century; they made little use of the traditional channels of labour and class struggle.

This most recent spate of protests against Macron's pension reform peaked in March 2023, when Macron forced the plan through without a parliamentary vote. This triggered a wave of strikes (including at oil terminals), the occupation of the Sorbonne, barricades on the streets, and riots in several cities. Resistance grew, and there were violent battles between police and protesters. The fight against pension reform slowly faded by May 2023, only to regain momentum in late June, when two police officers shot the seventeen-year-old Nahel Merzouk in a Paris suburb. The killing sparked a nationwide wave of riots and protests in late June 2023, when demonstrators not only attacked police stations and town halls but also set fire to a mayor's private residence. While in 2005 the suburban riots were largely confined to specific suburbs in Paris and Lyon, in 2023 they spread with explosive speed to a wide range of cities and neighbourhoods. Nor was it just suburban dwellers who took part in the protests; the crowd was far more diverse and much larger than in 2005. The government deployed 40,000 police and soldiers to quell the protests, which lasted more than a week.

Alongside these mass protests, there have been a number of long-term campaigns against major infrastructure projects in France.[8] Activists are fighting against both capitalist development and the state, to support nature and the right to decide how their local environment should look and be organized. One of the most important of these struggles was against the construction of an airport outside the city of Nantes. The €580 million construction project was approved in 2008 and should have begun in 2014 and been completed in 2017. But the plan was rejected from the outset by local farmers and activists, who entrenched themselves on the 1,650 ha site. From 2008 onwards, the area evolved into an experimental eco-anarchist utopia called the zone to defend (ZAD) of Notre-Dame-des-Landes, where locals and activists hailing from across France and Western Europe developed alternative ways of living ouside the money economy. More than 100 self-governed settlements sprang up, as well as a library, a bakery, a brewery and a radio station. Various forms of farming and animal husbandry sprang up too, including for goats and cows. On several occasions large detachments of police officers attempted unsuccessfully to clear the area, most recently in 2018, when police descended upon the zone with helicopters, armoured personnel carriers, water cannons and bulldozers. Police fired more than 8,000 teargas grenades and 300 stun grenades during the ten days in which they tried to clear the area in April 2018. When the airport project was finally dropped by the French government, some activists continued their fight. Joined by groups of small farmers, they initiated Les Soulèvements de la Terre, a direct action movement that focuses (among other things) on the sabotage or 'disarmament' of mega-basins, that is, large-scale water reservoir projects that make it possible for agro-industrial companies to appropriate and privatize water sources.

France is perhaps the best exemplification in Western Europe of the idea that we live in an 'age of revolt', as Donatella Di Cesare describes our times in a small but important book about contemporary revolts.[9] But the picture is the same in many other places. Take a country like Chile, where in May 2011 students occupied more than 800 high school and university buildings, in protest against the country's grossly unequal education system, which favours the children of wealthy parents, since they alone can pay the growing fees that are among the most expensive in the world. High school and university students dressed up as zombies and danced in front of the presidential palace in Santiago de Chile to Michael Jackson's 'Thriller'. Their meaning was unmistakable: the education system was turning them into the indebted living dead. The occupations of high schools were accompanied by the largest demonstrations to take place in the capital and other cities since the fall of the dictatorship.

The Piñera government continuously tried to take the wind out of the protesters' sails by convening so-called dialogue meetings. It also dismissed two ministers of education, while simultaneously allowing the police to use excessive force and *agents provocateurs*, that is, plainclothes police officers who incited not only destruction of property but also personal violence. The government tried to negotiate with various student organizations, but the students on the streets rejected any invitation to dialogue from the government. On 17 August 2011 the government presented a revised proposal for financing education, but it was rejected outright. In Santiago de Chile a two-day 'national citizen strike' led to violent clashes between the police and protesters, during which a sixteen-year-old student was shot in the head by a police officer in a passing car. In September, the students, dressed in all black, organized several large 'silent marches' through Santiago and other cities. From October on the government stepped up the repression, passing a law that would lead to imprisonment for the occupation of educational institutions and giving police free rein on the streets to use not only more tear gas but also water cannons. Faced with accelerated repression, many young people chose to return to their classes, while some continued to occupy their colleges or universities.

Although the last occupations were disbanded in early 2012, discontent against the government's neoliberal education policies continued to simmer, and on 17 November 2019 it erupted again in full force. In protest against higher metro ticket prices in the capital, high school students launched a campaign for free transport that quickly turned into large-scale street protests. The young people occupied and vandalized every metro station in Santiago, setting several ablaze along the way. But the discontent was by no means limited to the youth; hundreds of thousands of others took to the streets, in protest against the government and the political system. That night Piñera, by then re-elected, declared a state of emergency in Santiago and several other major cities and deployed the military. But the protests only continued and became more intense.

The Chilean philosopher Rodrigo Karmy describes the events in Santiago as a radical and unexpected rupture, as if a huge hole suddenly appeared in the middle of the road. 'Whatever happened to this date? Is it just a chronological date? Perhaps, a dislocated number that, while locating itself on a calendar, desperately flees from it. Its potency does not match its figures, its life with its letter. It explodes without referring to any leader, nor to any political party or partisan vanguard.'[10] The mass protests continued for days, with looting of shops and fierce fighting between the military and protesters; more than fifty lives were lost and thousands were arrested and imprisoned. A week after the protests started, more than 1 million people took to the streets of Santiago. While deploying the army, the government also tried to deflate the protests by replacing a number of ministers, cancelling the price hike on metro tickets, and even drafting a constitutional amendment. Even this failed to discourage the protesters, who refused to be channelled in a partisan direction, be it towards the government or towards the opposition. It was a rejection of both the right and the left in Chilean politics.

As Karmy writes, the protests dissolved the constituted power's claim to authority.[11] It was the political system as a whole that needed to be dismantled, not just the Piñera government. The proposed new constitution may have passed with a large majority in a referendum on 15 November 2020, but it wasn't the constitutional changes that killed the protests, it was the Covid-19 lockdown and the fear of having to pay for treatment in a country where healthcare is expensive.

France and Chile are but two examples of how mass protests continue to take place in a complex global flow, where specific local causes merge into a comprehensive rejection of the dominant order. One protest follows another, as if someone had finally managed to invent a perpetual motion machine. The protests in France and Chile over the past ten to fifteen years are part of a global narrative in which protesters constantly inspire one another, cross borders, and mobilize entire continents.

3

The New Movement

If protesters in Tunisia and Egypt attacked local dictators in 2011, in 2016 Nuit debout in France started to protest a planned labour market reform. If Extinction Rebellion blocked five bridges in London in 2018 to protest inaction on climate change, the George Floyd revolt in 2020 was fuelled by racialized police brutality in the United States. Many have rightly asked whether we can even use the same term for so many different sorts of protests.[1] Each time, there seem to be very specific local causes that bring people to the streets: in a nutshell, an injustice that turns frustration into anger and indignation. The list is long, but exemplary cases are Mohamed Bouazizi in Tunisia in 2010, Mark Duggan in the United

Kingdom in 2011, George Floyd in the United States in 2020, Giovanni López in Mexico the same year and Nahel Merzouk in France in 2023. Each of these direct or indirect state murders triggered a tidal wave of protest.

There have undoubtedly been significant differences between the many demonstrations, occupations and uprisings that have taken place since 2011, but most often the anger has been directed at the state, for one reason or another. The state raises the price of petrol or metro tickets or implements a pension reform, or a citizen dies in police custody. And once there are enough people on the streets, the protests grow and come to be about much more than the specific issue that triggered the protest in the first place. In most cases, the demands evolve into outright rejections of the state and the political order. Any random occasion can mobilize an explosive, unprogrammed anger.

As early as 2013, in a short book about the first phase of the new wave of protests, Michael Hardt and Antonio Negri wrote that, although 'each struggle was singular and orientated towards specific local conditions', taken together, all of them were nevertheless connected and constituted 'a new cycle of protest'.[2] As Hardt and Negri pointed out, these events referred to each other: Occupy referred to the 15-M movement in Spain, the 15-M referred to the Egyptian revolutionary masses gathered in Tahrir Square, and the Egyptian revolutionaries ordered pizzas for the park occupiers in Manhattan, just as the Syrian revolutionaries wrote statements of support for the Yellow Vests, explaining that 'our struggle is common. . . . You cannot be in favour of a revolution in Syria if you side with Macron.'[3]

On the streets, the connections have always been present in references and statements of support. In the context of the university occupations that took place in the spring of 2024 in the United States and a number of other countries, the connection is explicit: buildings and campuses are occupied in protest against local universities' financial interests, which favour companies that contribute to the occupation of the West Bank and the genocide in Gaza. Moreover, the new mass protests do have shared tactics, just as we saw in earlier historical periods; for example, the mass strike united the revolts of 1905, 1912 and 1917. In 2011 the square occupations spread from Cairo to Barcelona, Madrid, Athens, Rome,

London, and then on to New York, Oakland, Istanbul and farther.[4] The occupation of public or previously public spaces proved to be not only an effective way to challenge the ruling order but also an experiment in new methods of organizing a horizontal political community. In 2019 it was the frontliner tactic – barricades built from bins, building materials and metal barriers; the use of umbrellas against police pepper spray; and lasers deployed against surveillance cameras and drones – that was suddenly shared across borders and continents, from Hong Kong to Chile, Ecuador, France and Iraq, and then to the United States in 2020.[5]

As we can see from the maps drawn by Alain Bertho and at the Carnegie,[6] the mass protests resemble scattered flare-ups of the chronic fever of a crisis-ridden system. Things explode in one place, are crushed, then erupt somewhere else: 'Protests spread, acts of disobedience multiply, and clashes intensify', as Di Cesare writes.[7]

Even the lockdowns caused by the Covid-19 pandemic didn't fully quell the protests. The George Floyd revolt in the United States in the summer of 2020 offers the clearest proof: thousands of people took to the streets across the country, demonstrating against yet another racist case of police brutality, looting stores and establishing autonomous zones where police had no monopoly on violence. African Americans took the lead, but the uprising mobilized a broad resistance, 'with people of all colours and genders quickly joining [the uprising]', as Shemon Salam and Arturo Castillon write.[8] The reterritorializations of capital – not least race and gender – did not prevent the uprising from catching on, as has so often happened in the US context, where the class alliance between the white working class and the local capitalist class has consistently destroyed many attempts at revolt.

Every time when there is looting, as in the United States in the summer of 2020, and protesters fight with the police, as in Paris in 2019 or in Chile that same year, or when protesters take a square and hold it, as in Tahrir Square in Cairo in 2011, a new subject is produced. In this *movement of refusal* the divisions of late capitalism are momentarily cancelled through a common refusal. The fragmented universe of the spectacular commodity economy – in which all previously existing class affiliations and feelings of solidarity are replaced by precarious and ephemeral identities of all kinds, largely mediated by the commodity form – is suddenly blown to smithereens, and in its place another world opens up amid the old (dis)order. The identities and organizations that sustain the late capitalist social structure give way to something completely different, which is not based on pre-existing notions and experiences of class, race, gender or nationality.

The new mass protests should be understood not merely as the antithesis to the inefficacy of institutional representation or as a mechanical consequence of the economic inequalities that plague so many countries worldwide but also as a radical challenge to the received grammar of political action: a grammar rooted in notions of political democracy, civil society and social movements, as they developed in Western Europe and elsewhere, in the context of the post-war Fordist wage–productivity compromise, with its negotiations of income, purchasing power, and party political interests within the nation state. The movement of refusal takes place beyond the political parties of national democracy and their struggle for votes, beyond the trade unions' mediation of the class struggle, and out of sight of the endless array of spokesmen, commentators and experts. The revolts of our time take place beyond all manner of representational logic and classic organization.

The Italian philosopher and militant Marcello Tarì, a fellow traveller of Le Comité invisible (the Invisible Committee), has aptly described these protests as 'destituent'.[9] They seek to depose government leaders, prime ministers and presidents. When protesters took to the streets in Tunisia in January 2011, they chanted *Dégage!*, *Irhal!* and *Barra!*. They wanted Ben Ali gone; in French, Arabic and Tunisian the chorus was saying the same: fuck off! But this was not addressed just to him and his clan of corrupt lackeys, the Ben Ali and Trabelsi families; the protesters wanted to tear down the entire political regime, including the postcolonial order that kept the Tunisian masses in submission and misery. As Hamid Dabashi writes, the slogans were directed 'against domestic tyranny and globalized disempowerment alike'.[10] What was in question was not simply a new government, different leaders, or a redistribution of power, but the rejection of it all.

As protests began to spread to other North African and Middle Eastern countries in the spring of 2011, *Irhal!* expanded into *Ash-sha'b yurīd isqāṭ an-niẓām* ('People want the fall of the regime'). In Egypt, the slogan was not only shouted in Tahrir Square but also tagged on countless walls across Cairo and other cities. In Bahrain as well as in Yemen, Syria and Libya, it reverberated in demonstrations against the local dictators.

As Tarì writes, all the protests from 2011 onwards have been characterized by an unmistakable urge to challenge, overthrow and destroy the prevailing political representations without proposing new ones. It's not about replacing the current government or leader with others and thereby arriving at a better version of what we already have. It's about getting rid of all the leaders, including the most critical opposition leaders; fundamentally, it's about dismantling the need for leaders *tout court*.

Refusal is a political act, yet it is neither class struggle in the traditional sense nor an attempt to establish some formal opposition to the constituted powers; instead it assumes the form of a violent rage against reality. In this sense, what is taking shape in the many protests around us is an anthropological showdown as much as a political one: an attempt to break free from all traditional notions of how the social context we call a society and a nation state is to be organized. For more and more people, it has become clear that it is not possible to deal with the many crises that continue to develop within the framework of contemporary political institutions, the climate crisis being perhaps the most obvious example.

Tarì finds the germ of the new protests in what is known as the Argentinazo: the Argentine uprising of December 2001, when millions of Argentines demanded the removal or ejection of the current local government. *Que se vayan todos!* ('They all have to go!') rang out in the streets of Buenos Aires, Rosario and other major cities. After more than a decade of market capitalist austerity and an economy of corrupt privatization led by the unpopular Minister of Economy Domingo Cavallo, who was highly regarded by the International Monetary Fund (IMF) and could therefore stay in office even when power changed hands, tensions finally reached boiling point. On 19 December 2001 tens of thousands took to the streets, initiating a massive wave of lootings. President Fernando de la Rúa declared a state of emergency in the early evening; shortly after midnight Cavallo resigned. But the unrest continued into the next day. De la Rúa tried to prevent national media from reporting on the protests, but to no avail; and eventually he, too, resigned, not before delivering a speech to the nation in which he tried to quell the resistance by proposing a new, broad-based government.

Tarì reads the 2001 uprising in Argentina as a harbinger of the new cycle of protest that began in 2011. The demonstrators in Buenos Aires and other cities in Argentina flatly rejected any attempt to limit the resistance to the matter of a different government or a new president. If it was a destituent uprising, this is because people on the streets were not just totally uninterested in a softer version of the IMF's austerity policies, they also discarded the very idea of bringing the political opposition to power. It was the entire political–economic system they were reacting against. This uprising was different. As the Argentine Colectivo Situaciones (Situations Collective) writes in an analysis that Tarì draws on, 'the movement of the 19th and 20th was more a de-instituting action than a classic instituting movement'.[11] The protesters rejected not only the de la Rúa government and the unpopular finance minister, but also all other politicians. As Colectivo

Situaciones writes, the protesters refused to play the role of the people.[12] They rejected both the existing order and the idea of establishing a new order in its place. In this way, what the protests enacted was less a counterpower than the absence of power. 'The revolt was violent. Not only did it topple a government and confront the repressive forces for hours. There was something more: it tore down the prevailing political representations without proposing others.'[13]

Following Colectivo Situaciones, Tarì ascribes to the new, paradoxical uprisings a desire to void power. Whenever a proposal for a new government, a new president or a new policy is formulated, the masses in the streets respond with a resounding 'No!'. The protests seem to take place beyond any notion of hegemony; they reject any attempt to represent and direct the discontent. What is perplexing to the existing order is this refrain, in which there is no question of either forming a new government or conquering state power. Confronted by protesters who challenge the ruling order not in order to take power themselves, but simply to refuse it, the entire modern political paradigm begins to disintegrate.

4

Refusal

We can describe the new protests as a *blank* refusal. Such was the gesture of Maurice Blanchot when he refused the circumstances in which Charles de Gaulle became president in France – a gesture that so impressed Marcuse, as we have seen.[1] Blanchot is not just refusing de Gaulle and all his co-conspirators – that is, all those working behind the scenes to get him back into the presidency, be they military personnel who refused to leave Algeria and threatened to invade France or people who just wanted the old general back. Blanchot refuses the whole political game that makes both the continued colonization of Algeria and the French Republic possible. We can see a similar refusal of the entire political system in the new protests: a refusal of all the representations of politics in circulation, including the many attempts to draw up political compromises and agreements designed to maintain the ruling order. As in the case of Blanchot's refusal of 1958, if there is anything political in the new protests, it lies in the rejection of ordinary politics as a site of fiddling, delays and political agreements. This refusal does not appeal to any universal normative values, nor does it propose alternative programmes and solutions. The refusal is not a call for more negotiations or new agreements – such as the Fifth Republic in 1958, Macron's 'great national debate' of 2019 or a new constitution in Chile today – but a form of total critique that both rejects the perpetual discussions about who should be leader and opposes all power.

Refusal is absolute: it does not invite negotiation, nor does it propose anything. For those who refuse, there is no compromise. As Blanchot writes: 'At a certain moment, when faced with public events, we know that we must refuse. Refusal is absolute, categorical. It does not discuss or voice its reasons. That is how it remains silent and solitary, even when it affirms itself, as it should, in broad daylight.'[2] For Blanchot, refusal was not a commitment to the political, as if to change this or that condition in society. It was a cancellation of the very logic of representation that characterizes modern politics. It is this silent, Blanchotian refusal that we find at work in the new mass protests, when they make no reference to pre-existing and recognizable political subjects, but simply take place.

Refusal is anonymous: if it is not the expression of a subject or an identity, this is because, as Blanchot observes, it is carried out from 'a very poor beginning that belongs first of all to those who cannot speak'.[3] Its consistency is the echo of the suffering of this world. One might think it easy to refuse; on the contrary, Blanchot insists, it is extremely difficult. For refusal refuses not only 'the worst but also a reasonable semblance, a solution that will be deemed happy and even unhoped for'.[4] So refusal is not only a refusal of what is happening – an instance of police violence, the poisoning of the earth, a genocide, new cuts or tax relief for the super-rich and so on – things that everyone ought to be against. It is also a refusal of the reasons that justify these processes, explain them away or neutralize them – of all the arguments for new negotiations, compromises, reconciliations.

With Giorgio Agamben, we can call what emerged in the streets of the United States in 2020, in France and Chile in 2019 and in many other places 'a coming community'.[5] Such a community is characterized neither by belonging nor by the absence of belonging, but is belonging nonetheless. Refusal does not create a political community. There is no positive identity that unites the many on the street: they are not a class, a nation or a people. The starting point for this community is always, in Paris as in Santiago and Minneapolis, the refusal of state organization. This is why we can say that it is a movement of refusal, a refusalist international, that we see emerging in all the protests. It is a movement that refuses the state as well as the economy that the state facilitates and maintains through its police, laws and regulations.

Marx made a distinction between the formal and the historical party; similarly, we can speak of mass protests as the *party of refusal*.[6] Of course, this is not a party in the everyday sense of a political party with members and a programme, like the German Social Democratic Party or the US

Republican Party (GOP), for instance. Indeed, it is a party precisely against such parties: it is a sub-party or an under-party, which emerges in and through a refusal of the whole world that 'real' parties represent and maintain when they fight to distribute the minimal leftovers of the economy.

We can call this new type of party an 'extra-political party of the ones who are none', to use Fred Moten's formulation.[7] It is born on the streets, during a protest, in a riot, or while people are looting, taking cover from police teargas or setting fire to a metro station. Its emergence takes the form of a spontaneous gathering. There is organization, there are people doing something together, but doing something completely different from what a political party or a trade union does, or what happens in a workplace. As Moten says, this party is new because it is not political in the usual sense: 'this is the new political party to end all political parties'.[8] And, most importantly, the new party doesn't have any members, you can't formally join it or be accepted as a new member, get a position, maybe even rise through the ranks to leadership. In the new under-party no one represents anyone. It's not something you join, it's something you do. And nothing whatsoever relates to representation in this party. There is no one to speak on behalf of someone else, and there is no formulated programme to betray or follow.

5

Aphasia

It can be extremely difficult to recognize the movement of refusal or the new sub-party in the many protests. Many otherwise sympathetic analyses mistake the protests for something that they are not. One of the main criticisms of the new mass protests is that they have not led to any major changes anywhere, and in many cases have even resulted in more misery and greater unfreedom – as for example in Egypt and Tunisia, where the 2011 ousting of the local dictators Ben Ali and Hosni Mubarak ended in an even worse iteration of the same, in the form of Kais Saied and Abdel Fattah al-Sisi.[1] Obviously, it should come as no surprise that the ruling order has done everything it could to derail the mass protests.

Revolutionary uprisings have always met with enormous repression or have been swept away by a counter-revolutionary movement that often presented itself as a response to discontent, while quietly angling to preserve the existing property relations and, if need be, to establish new ruling classes.

Another common criticism of the new protest movements is that they themselves are not clear about what they really want and have no programme of any kind. They want all sorts of things, but nothing in particular. In a small book entitled *La destitution du peuple*, the linguist Jean-Claude Milner, also a former Maoist, writes that the Yellow Vests, who occupied the roundabouts of France for more than fourteen months, had no language in which to make political demands to the Macron government and the political establishment.[2] The protesters, Milner argues, did not seem interested in achieving anything political with their occupations and protests. They were interested in something else. What was that? – asks Milner. Why did they occupy roundabouts in the provinces and attack restaurants in the city centre of Paris? Why did hundreds of thousands of people who, according to surveys, had never participated in demonstrations or been politically active before suddenly take to the streets? Milner's answer comes a little sourly: nobody knows – neither the many who have analysed the protests nor, even worse, the many who took part in them.

Milner describes this situation as an absence of language. The protesters rejected the idioms of trade unions and political parties. They lined up at roundabouts and on country roads, stole photos of Macron from local town halls and walked around with them upside down. The result was a kind of aphasia, Milner writes.[3] The situation was such that many protesters seemed unable to articulate what they were protesting against, or what the protests were actually trying to achieve. This, Milner concludes, amounts to a linguistic breakdown: the Yellow Vests were unable to communicate with the media or the ruling order – and, even worse, with each other. It was difficult to find the right words, as if the place where words are formed had been damaged. The Yellow Vests did not have access to a political vocabulary. The protesters were incapable of articulating what they wanted and why they were in the streets in the first place.

If the Yellow Vests communicated anything, it was, according to Milner, a kind of 'general complaint' or objection directed at all sorts of different issues. Therefore the complaint exceeded what the political order could possibly understand, he writes. And, anyway, this complaint was not so much a political complaint or a criticism of specific political, social or economic issues, but rather a simultaneous collapse and expansion of all the specific complaints that could be voiced. The result was a strangely abstract and blank dissatisfaction with everything. As Milner puts it, '[i]n reality, it [sc. the Yellow Vests' complaint] condemns everything that stands in the way of life'.[4] If, throughout history – that is, during the past 200 years in France – trade unions, parties and social movements have made specific demands in order to compromise on the division of society – say, more pay and less work, or access to education and culture – the Yellow Vests did no such thing.

Milner does not specify whether 'aphasia' in his characterization of the Yellow Vests is meant to be taken as anomic aphasia, that is, the inability to find words for objects – in this case, to express discontent and put it into words – or maybe to describe an even worse situation, where the protesters themselves do not understand the meaning of their protests. Either way, Milner sees in these protests the expression of a deeper crisis that confronts France and that the Yellow Vests served to intensify. The aphasia of the Yellow Vests is a metaphor for a political collapse in which the people is disintegrating as a political subject. Hence the title of Milner's book: the destitution of the people.

6

The End of Reformism

Milner is undoubtedly a bit know-it-all, if not downright patronizing, but he manages to put into words a vague sense of surprise and disappointment that many have expressed when confronted with the numerous mass protests that have taken place since Mohamed Bouazizi set himself on fire, on 17 December 2010, in the Tunisian provincial town of Sidi Bouzid. Of course, many audiences were extremely enthusiastic when Ben Ali, Tunisia's president, was overthrown, as they were when thousands occupied Tahrir Square in Cairo in late January 2011 and managed to force Mubarak to step down. Soon after, inspired by the events in Tunisia and Egypt, demonstrators took to the streets in

Spain and Greece to protest against the massive national austerity programmes implemented in the wake of the financial crisis. During the summer and autumn of 2011, cities in Europe and North America were the scene of mass protests, occupations and riots.

After decades of what Mark Fisher called 'capitalist realism', during which it was impossible to imagine anything other than the optimization of neoliberal capitalism and its systems of governance, the events of 2011 were a breath of fresh air, a break with the slow transformation of politics into 'consensual administration'.[1]

For a long time in the West, mass protests were something that took place elsewhere, more specifically in what was once called the Second World and the Third World. Protesting was something that groups of people did in order to get what we in the West had – as when East German citizens tore down the Berlin Wall in 1989. Events like the fall of the Berlin Wall seemed to confirm that, at least in the West, revolutions were a thing of the past. Of course, in the period since 1989 there were demonstrations even in the West, but neither the alter-globalization movement of the late 1990s nor the large anti-war demonstrations against the invasion of Iraq in 2003 really got off the ground; and they certainly failed to burst the neoliberal consensus. The alter-globalization movement was brutally crushed in a test run of the counter-insurgency regime installed after 9/11. The events in Genoa in July 2001 during the G8 summit where Carlo Giuliani was shot dead and hundreds of protesters severely beaten up by Italian police showed the capability and willingness of the system to repress any anti-systemic protest even before 9/11. The attacks on the World Trade Center and the Pentagon only seemed to reinforce the West's self-image as the cradle of democracy – and the end of history, now that it confronted the threat of a retrograde Islamism. When asked if he was surprised that millions took to the streets across the world, to protest the impending invasion of Iraq, George W. Bush smilingly explained to reporters: 'This is what we are exporting to Iraq.'[2]

The year 2011 was a very different story. Western media did try to frame the Arab Spring as a narrative about Western democracy's reaching less developed countries, but this proved somewhat difficult, not merely because Western governments were only too eager to help local dictators crush the uprisings – Nicolas Sarkozy's foreign minister revealingly offered to send paratroopers to Tunisia to quell the 'unrest' – but also because young people, first in Southern Europe but quickly also in the United States and many other places in the West, began occupying squares and protesting bank bailouts and austerity, while explicitly referring to the revolts in North Africa and the Middle East.

Since January 2011 we have had demonstrations, occupations, riots and revolts. As Vincent Bevins writes, the early 2010s witnessed a veritable explosion in the number of mass protests – a fragmented yet global anti-system movement.[3] The protests have been so widespread that both 2011 and 2019 have been labelled 'a new May '68', and in 2011 the magazine *Time* chose the figure of the protester as 'person of the year'.[4] In the summer of 2020, the venerable capitalist magazine *The Economist* explained that 'political protests have become more widespread and more frequent', while also warning its readers that 'the rising trend of global unrest is likely to continue'.[5]

Representatives of the global bourgeoisie – in this case the Deutsche Bank research team – saw the writing on the wall, announcing in a 2020 report that we were entering 'an age of disorder'.[6] Despite these warnings, it has proven difficult for the global bourgeoisie to develop a coherent programme for restructuring the world economy. The ruling classes seem unable to agree on a plan, either globally or locally. Green transition, protectionism or further globalization? Brexit and Trump's presidency are testament to the accelerating *infighting* among the ruling class.

Today it would be hard for the situationist Gianfranco Sanguinetti to pass himself off as an anonymous influential industrialist who leaks plans on how the Italian bourgeoisie will save capitalism by staging anarchist terrorist attacks and false flag operations.[7] Everyone knows there is no plan. While tech billionaires might dream of moving to Mars, large parts of the local capitalist classes just want 'four more years', Biden or Harris, while others have readied themselves for command economy initiatives and huge investments in military equipment, even if all this comes with the political leadership of the new fascists.

The dream of green capitalism is hanging by a thread. Geopolitical disputes are increasing, the economic crisis is now taking the form of inflation, and none of the usual solutions is really working: higher interest rates, lower or higher taxes, stimuli, or curbing private consumption. The underlying consensus seems to be that capital must be destroyed before it can be relaunched. Israel appears as the archetype of a new political–economic solution: rather than containing and imprisoning the Palestinian surplus population in Gaza, just bomb it to pieces. Investments in military hardware and all manners of counter-insurgency equipment have exploded in recent years.[8] Covid-19 lockdowns have given states additional powers to monitor and control populations.[9] In sum, there is no indication that we will see less conflict and repression in the coming years.

More and more people seem ready to resort to violence, not least in the United States, where it looks like every housewife in Florida is a rabid anti-woke Oath Keeper and many businessmen are armed Proud Boys ready to help Trump or another fascist leader clean up the country and 'Make America Great Again'. Heated culture wars, often staged as generational clashes, are just the tip of the iceberg. Underneath, we have a capitalism that cannot act strategically in the face of an accelerating climate crisis and stalling growth – and in most economies growth never really returned after 2008. Wherever we look, the objective conditions for more protests are growing.[10] We are in a situation where the molecules of society are being ionized, as Bordiga would put it.[11]

7

Anti-Politics

The return of mass protests was greeted with enthusiasm by many on the left, especially those with an eye for the structural violence that the capitalist mode of production necessarily entails and that has only increased in recent decades, whether in the form of exploitation and exclusion of people or destruction of nature and biodiversity. After forty years of neoliberal restructuring, Washington Consensus and 'end of history', many welcomed the sight of demonstrations and struggles in the streets. Spontaneous refusals in the guise of local gestures (e.g. Bouazizi's suicide) could suddenly trigger massive mobilizations of anger, but in the end these either evaporated suddenly or were brutally smothered by the police.

People kept going to the streets now here now there, but it was as if the protests never really got off the ground; they just kept failing. It seemed almost impossible to sustain a continuous struggle for longer. There was no shortage of tactical innovations – the *cortège de tête* [front bloc] was just one out of many – but coherent programmes or unifying international horizons were hard to find. The overall mood was characterized by desperation rather than hope or belief in something better. There was no positive political horizon.

How are we to understand this absence, this refusal of politics? Some, for instance Milner, criticize the protests for failing to embody modern mass politics and for *draining* instead the constitutive political subject of its signifying impetus, when its task is to transcend specific sociological identities. Others, such as the art historian T. J. Clark, a short-lived member of the Situationist International, observe with despair how the young people who looted sneakers and iPhones during the riots that took place in London, Birmingham and Manchester in the summer of 2011 in response to the killing of Mark Duggan by the police were completely unable to engage critically with the spectacular commodity society.[1] Clark is not without sympathy for the young people who looted sports shops and shopping centres, but he sees in such acts a form of political resignation. According to the old situationist, acts of looting display a deep nihilism. Young people set fire to their own neighbourhoods, looted sports shops, and played games with the police, but it all took place without much commitment. It was, at best, a chance to burn some steam. According to Clark, these youngsters had no hope that their actions would mean anything or make any difference. The rejection of a racist police force that controls communities at the margins of the commodity economy occurs in the absence of notions of genuine transgression. Young people fight the police and steal iPhones, hoodies, sneakers and pizzas but have no concept of access to another, possibly better world, whether through the invisible hand of the market or an organized socialist offensive. They are stuck and have no way out. The police will always be there to control them, and there will always be new generations of iPhones to get hold of, steal or buy, so it just goes on and on.

Clark sees an abyssal emptiness in young people who run in and out of shops or try to set cars on fire in London and Birmingham. They no longer believe in the commodity economy's promises of quick happiness – the next mobile phone, a pair of Nike Travis Scott Jumpman Jack shoes, or a Tesla Cybertruck – yet neither do they have access to the vision of a different world, without police and price form. They are stuck once in a while looting shops, even though they no longer believe in the quick identity fix of the spectacular commodity economy. The constantly flashing screens no longer reveal anything desirable, but there is nothing else, so young people perform their meaningless gestures of refusal that point nowhere. They can't get away, they are trapped. 'Cleaning out the Pizza Hut was *not* exciting', Clark writes.[2]

If the Watts race riots of 1965, which Debord and the situationists analysed in their journal *Internationale situationniste*, contained a glimpse of another world, the looting of the Bull Ring Shopping Centre in Birmingham had no such dimension; there was neither another world nor a world upside down.[3] The looting in 2011 was nothing more than a 'miserable insurrection', the old situationist writes.⁴ Over £200 million worth of damage was done and thousands of trainers, mobile phones and pizzas were distributed 'for free' among the youths of the neighbourhood, but the fundamental sadness of it all was never overcome.

Unsure how to grasp what he calls the 'absence of politics' in the protests, Clark winds up positioning himself outside them; he finds in them nothing but 'the spectacle of consumerism obediently devouring its own tail'.⁵ Such phrases cannot be uttered without a tinge of disgust. Clark naturally wants the nihilism of young people to be seen as an expression of the emptiness of the spectacular commodity economy – 'the last trace of belief in the pseudo-paradise of goods had deserted its shock troops'⁶ – but he ends up relegating them to an infinite hall of mirrors where it is impossible to distinguish between the destruction of the spectacle and the spectacle of destruction.

It is a story of defeat. Like Milner, Clark describes protesters on the street as extras, people who participate in something they have no real influence over. Those who occupy roundabouts in rural France or attack the Arc de Triomphe in Paris are without agency, they suffer from aphasia, writes Milner. Clark describes the young people who battle racist police in London and Birmingham as 'just another element in the media continuum'.[7] In other words, young people were as disengaged in their rebellion as they were in everything else in their lives. For both Milner and Clark, the protesters and rioters act without any political consciousness; they riot and protest, but do it without any political purpose to speak of.

8

The Workers' Movement

Milner and Clark are certainly right to note an absence in the new mass protests. Unfortunately they understand this absence as a lack, as either aphasia or nihilism. This explains why their analyses are so pessimistic: both overlook the novelty of the mass protests, their attempts to develop a completely different type of political action, unlike the programmes and tactics handed down from the twentieth-century workers' movement, the revolutionary decolonial movements after the Second World War or the social movements of the final decades of that century. The movement of refusal is something different. The problem is that these two ageing revolutionaries, like many others who have sought to analyse the new cycle of protest, remain stuck in the past and blame the people on the streets for not fulfilling the revolutionary ideals of previous generations. In doing so, Milner and Clark not only perpetuate a model that no longer exists; they also miss the experimentation with new political practices that takes place under their very eyes and that reaches beyond both sovereignist and representational models. The new mass protests refuse the existing order and do not propose any other in its stead.

An important aspect of the analysis of the new mass protests is the weathering of the conditions of possibility for an earlier language of protest, which the workers' movement developed throughout the twentieth century and which played a central role in the revolutionary and reformist challenges to the local capitalist classes in Europe, but also on other continents. In Marxist terms, at issue here is a transformation of the class struggle and of the capital–labour relationship.

Following an analysis made by the French left-communist group Théorie Communiste, the Endnotes collective has described this development as a history of the dissolution of the factory.[1] We are dealing with a long and twisted narrative, in which the relationship between capital and labour changes and the political power of the working class slowly disappears. From the mid-nineteenth century until the 1970s, the factory was the place where the people or nation of the future was created. It was the factory worker who would open the door to 'historical society' (in the Marxist sense), by abolishing capitalism and putting an end to 'prehistory'. However, with the transition to the new regime of accumulation in the 1970s and 1980s, the basis for this vision disappeared. Milner and Clark are of course aware of this development, but seem unable to come to terms with it.

According to the various strands of socialist theory, the political power of the working class was only supposed to grow. If we recall Marx and Engels' description in *The Communist Manifesto*, the idea was that the development of capitalism would lead to a polarization of society: a small minority of capital owners and a large majority of wage workers would end up facing each other.[2] The other classes would slowly disappear and be absorbed into the proletariat. The result of this development would be a revolution in which the political power of the capitalist class over society was abolished and the capitalist mode of production dismantled and replaced by a communist mode; and in the communist society that followed impersonal market forces and the demands of capital accumulation would disappear.

The goal of socialism was the abolition of capitalism and wage labour. As wage labourers, workers were a dominated class that was forced to submit to the rule of capital and to the capitalist class. In order to survive, the worker had to sell his or her labour power. The revolution attempted the reversal of this situation. Profit-driven production was to be replaced by production that satisfied the wants and needs of workers. The chaos of the market economy was to be replaced by a mode of production that was planned and anchored in the collective and conscious decisions of workers.

Marx and Engels' *Manifesto of the Communist Party*, written in the run-up to the 1848 revolutions, was an early attempt to give the workers' movement a language and a programme. The two young hotspurs (who did not sign the first editions of the *Manifesto*: a historical detail worth remembering)[3] explain there that modern society is a class society in which capital has the upper hand, exploiting the proletariat's labour power and producing ever more sums of money, which the capitalists then reinvest in the system. The dramatic description of the dismantling of feudal social structures under the capitalist mode of production – 'all that is solid melts into air' – culminates in the description of the decisive duel: the struggle between the bourgeoisie and the proletariat. As Marx explained later, in the tens of thousands of pages he wrote attempting to construct a coherent critique of political economy, capital can reproduce itself only by intensifying the labour of the proletariat. There is an inherent contradiction between capital and labour, between those who own the means of production and those who produce. The class struggle is an expression of this contradiction. The problem with the capitalist class is that it depends upon the labour power of the proletariat for the creation of value, but at the same time is compelled to get rid of the proletariat, which demands too much and represents a costly expense. In this way capital is constantly in the process of cutting off the branch upon which it sits. The proletariat holds the keys: although it is subordinate to capital in the production process, it is, according to Marx and Engels, the historical class destined to overcome this contradiction.

Referring to the decisive struggles of the proletariat at the time, Marx and Engels not only drew up a critical analysis but also concluded their short work with two demands that constituted a kind of communist programme of action: the abolition of private property; and internationalism. For almost a century and a half, armed with an often dubious reference to Marx, the workers' movement struggled to build a different world out of the old agrarian societies fractured by turbulent capitalist modernization. In the final stage of the revolutionary period of the bourgeoisie leading up to 1848, it was extremely difficult for the working class to organize itself. Both the old order and the bourgeoisie intensely combatted any attempt at working-class self-organization. In the nineteenth century, each time the working class revolted, it was brutally suppressed; the Paris Commune of 1871 stands as a prime example of this fate.

In the decades after the Commune, a process of large-scale organization began in earnest and the workers' movement quickly grew into a formidable political force. At the same time it split into a revolutionary and a reformist part. This split would continue throughout the twentieth century, from the rapid rise of labour parties through popular uprisings and revolutions to world wars and crises. Later on it led to the establishment of parliamentary democracies in the highly developed industrial world and to the expropriation of the capitalist classes in what was known as the socialist camp – the Soviet Union and its various satellites – after the end of the Second World War. The aim of the various sections of the labour movement was still to socialize the production, but according to the revisionist socialists this had to be done through the legal means provided by bourgeois society.

Throughout the twentieth century the various segments of the workers' movement debated how the class struggle ought to be conducted. But, as the left communists of Théorie Communiste have described, both the revolutionary and the reformist wings of the workers' movement imagined that more and more workers would eventually take power one way or another and reorganize production, so that their class would be at the helm.[4] In spite of their differences at other levels, all factions shared the vision of workers' power.

The different models of transition, both reformist and revolutionary, all subscribed to the idea of socializing production.

Across many heated debates over how best to fight capitalism, virtually all the factions of the workers' movement were convinced that the factory was the starting point for the transformation. The lever for revolutionary transformation, be it achieved through councils, elections or the dictatorship of the proletariat, was the ever-growing industrial proletariat. Marx and Engels had laid out this perspective in the *Manifesto*, describing how capitalist industrialization would draw ever more workers into factories. 'The development of Modern industry . . . cuts from under its feet the very foundation on which the bourgeoisie produces and appropriates products.'[5] As more and more proletarians end up as wage labourers in factories, the working class would grow stronger. 'The advance of industry, whose involuntary promoter is the bourgeoisie, replaces the isolation of the laborers, due to competition, by the revolutionary combination, due to association', as Marx and Engels optimistically put it.[6]

In the *Manifesto*, the proletariat was identified with industrial workers in large factories.

The more of them there were, the stronger the working class would be in the class struggle.[7] The factory was the starting point for a new society, a socialist or communist society that was pressing upon the existing world. Big industry dissolved previous classes and produced more and more workers. At some point they would be so many that the revolution would materialize. Either there would be enough of them to make it possible to launch comprehensive reforms through elections, or workers would rise up in revolt, take control of the factories and dismantle the economic and political power of the capitalist class. Either way, the factory was the starting point of the new society: at the assembly line the workers became the proletariat – the unique historical subject that would build a new world.

All the various socialist and communist factions of the workers' movement were united in seeing industrialization as the way forward. Everyone is familiar with the storied images of big, strong factory workers: they became a crucial feature of working-class political culture for much of the twentieth century. It was this figure that took centre stage in visions of industrialization, class struggle and revolution. Factory workers, here in the present, were the people of the future. Most often they were depicted as a plurality, as in Diego Rivera's many murals, in which workers look proudly and self-confidently aware of their common mission as they stand next to one another, carrying recognizable tools – hammers, sickles, but also rifles and books – in buildings they are collectively constructing. Other times they appeared as individuals, acting as impressive (or oppressive) role models for all the other workers – as did Stakhanov, who one day in 1935 made a special effort for the new Soviet experiment and exceeded his daily work norm by 1,300 per cent.

In short, the workers' movement played a crucial role, for more than a century, as the most powerful immanent critique of modern capitalist society. As it was a child of this society, its various segments attempted to dismantle or expand this same society in a progressive direction. Historians and sociologists such as Geoff Eley, Michael Denning and Göran Therborn have described in detail how the established workers' movement was a crucial driving force in the development of the post-war democratic welfare state, where large parts of the lower classes in the West gained access to education, cultural activities and, last but not least, permanent jobs with a relatively stable salary.[8] The transformation of the hell of the factory into something less nightmarish and the extension of political rights to a majority of the population in the West and in many other parts of the world were achievements of the workers' movement. In a nutshell, they were the result of class struggle.

But this is also the story of how the established workers' movement was led to act opportunistically and to forget all those subjected to racial–colonial violence. That's why Aimé Césaire felt compelled to resign from the French Communist Party in 1956: the party either could not or would not understand that the colonial question should not be subordinated to the question of the industrial working class in France and that coloured subjects were also part of the proletariat.[9] The difficulty the workers' movement displayed in dealing with this issue was surpassed only by the reluctance to address the violence and oppression of women. As generations of Marxist feminists repeatedly stressed, from Clara Zetkin to Silvia Federici, it was extremely difficult for the workers' movement to move beyond the confines of the factory and see the home as the basis of the factory system.[10] The story of the tremendous success of the workers' movement is in fact so tarnished that it threatens to become the story of one disastrous blind spot after another.

9

The Socialist Horizon and Beyond

The workers' movement emerged in the final decades of the nineteenth century as an organized socialist movement endowed with a radical political perspective. As a subversive and capital-negating project, it died quietly in the period after the Second World War, then made a brief reappearance on the streets, after the last great proletarian offensive of the years 1968–1977. It proved very difficult to be consistently revolutionary and anti-capitalist in capitalist society; as a result, the workers' movement was constantly pressed into using given social processes to achieve limited goals. However, after the anti-fascist struggle of the interwar period, which saw broad collaborations between socialist and bourgeois parties, the workers' movement very rarely acted revolutionarily anywhere, and least of all in the metropolises of capital.

In retrospect we are forced to conclude, with Mario Tronti, that it was in fact post-war political national democracy that slowly killed the workers' movement by draining it of its remaining revolutionary energy.[1] After two world wars and a major economic crisis, when the welfare state replaced free competitive capitalism, the organized workers' movement was slowly incorporated into the state. After the Thirty Years War of the twentieth century, the people were finally united into a people – a nation. As Tronti writes, the masses were thus transformed from an internationalist collective into national working classes that no longer threatened the economy.[2] Their members were now recognized as legitimate political subjects, were paid more for being more productive – and, importantly, were more *docile*, refraining from any collective revolutionary activity. This temporarily resolved the conflict between labour and capital; and the threat of a workers' uprising that had haunted the ruling classes after the October Revolution in Russia and failed revolutions, in Germany in particular, was dismantled. Local workers were given more pay, as well as access to the ballot box, and the representatives of the working class slowly abandoned the idea of workers' power.

The history of the German Social Democrats exemplifies this development of anti-systemic implosion. After an extensive discussion in the late nineteenth century about the 'neutrality' of the state and the pitfalls of parliamentary democracy, the party ran for the Reichstag, and in 1914 a majority of its representatives voted in favour of German participation in the First World War. Things went downhill from there, and in January 1919 Chancellor Friedrich Ebert, the leader of the Social Democratic Party, authorized the suppression of the communist Spartacist uprising, an event in which the young Marcuse took part. Henceforth the line was drawn. It quickly became more important for socialist parties and the official workers' movement to secure their own growth than to fight for the revolutionary overthrow of capitalism. Thus, throughout the twentieth century, most socialist and communist parties sought to dampen the rebellious energy of the dangerous classes. The behaviour of the French Communist Party in May–June 1968 is only the most famous example of this unfortunate turn.³

While there were still self-identified revolutionary organizations in many countries in Western Europe and elsewhere, most of them were usually mired in misplaced faith in a Soviet Union that had fairly quickly opted for party dictatorship and state capitalism. This did not stop the Soviet regime and its staunch supporters from continuing to refer to Marx, socialism and communism almost to the end. In reality, however, 'real socialism' or 'actually existing socialism' (the formula used in the Eastern Bloc countries) had quickly abandoned the task of putting an end to the compulsion of capital accumulation and of dismantling the class structure of the vanquished capitalist society. Russia's aristocracy and bourgeoisie were replaced by a new upper class of party bureaucrats in the Soviet Union. Guy Debord writes: 'The revolutionary bureaucracy, which placed itself at the head of the proletariat, seized the State and proceeded to impose a new form of class rule on society.'⁴

The social movements of the New Left in the late 1950s and the 1960s came out as the final offshoot of the workers' movement. They rejected state capitalism in the East and mocked the culturally reactionary societies of the West, but operated with the idea of a different management of production that nevertheless continued to work within the existing communist horizon of taking power. Stuart Hall's extremely detailed conjunctural analyses and interventions in the public debate in Britain, for example, were always carried out with reference to Labour and within the framework of the existing political public sphere.[5] Even the creative segments of the 1977 autonomous movement in Italy, which went quite far in its experiments, continued to make fun of the workers' movement, socialist parties and Marxism. And the ferocity with which Carla Lonzi abandoned art criticism and Marxism in favour of a radical separatist feminism is a testament to the importance that Marxism still had in the early 1970s.[6] The new mass protests – the movement of refusal – take place at a distance from this socialist horizon: they are no longer about the workers' affirming or negating themselves in order to establish workers' power as an alternative to the bourgeoisie, finance capital or private property.

The underlying reason for this shift lies in the reorganization of the relationship between capital and labour that took place throughout the 1970s and 1980s.[7] The shift dismantled the Fordist regime of accumulation, which had begun to run out of steam in the late 1960s as a result of internal challenges, but not least because of the repeated attacks that militant workers, youths, feminists and migrants had directed against it throughout the 1960s.

The search for profit now took on a new form with the privatization of public industry, the gradual dismantling of the welfare state, the relocation of jobs and the precarization of much of the work that replaced the compromises of Keynesianism in the old centre. One of the consequences of what we often call, in a misleading shorthand, 'neoliberal globalization' has been a dramatic intensification of the process of separation that capital always entails, whereby workers are separated from one another. This atomization has resulted in the final disintegration of the working class as a political–economic as well as oppositional subject. If the workers' movement institutionally dismantled itself as an anti-systemic force in the post-war period, the worker as class consciousness has now also been dissolved.

In retrospect, it is clear that the period from the late nineteenth century to the mid-1970s was the heyday of the worker. But restructuring is not only the dissolution of a previous paradigm; it is also the birth of a new period, which means the eruption of new struggles. This is what we witness in the movement of refusal. It is no longer a struggle for more pay, longer holidays or better working conditions; it is a more radical struggle, designed to stop the violence of the state and to detach itself from the capital–labour relationship. It is no longer a struggle for representation, in which the working class strives to be represented politically. The unity that this struggle presupposed no longer exists – the working class as a unified entity is no more. The recent mobilization of the national working class by today's newfangled fascists is the perverse expression of this development. It is only as a simulacrum that the worker exists today. And if he or she does, it is in the form of violent white resentment. It therefore no longer makes sense to formulate wage demands that unite workers in trade unions, and then to implement these demands as political programmes, through parties in a national democracy. This whole complex, which was once intended to produce the working class as a subject with common interests (and aware of them), no longer exists. This working class has been blown to pieces through precarization and international competition.

This is why so many of the new mass protests are directed against the state. The sphere of production is no longer the site where the working class gathers and fights. Joshua Clover has helpfully described this shift as a transition from strikes to riots.[8] The numerous occupations of central squares in cities or roundabouts in the countryside are an expression of this situation, where the rejection of the ruling order and of the miserable state of the world takes place in the sphere of circulation. As the left communist Paul Mattick wrote in the early 1970s, the modern state, whatever its form, is essentially a capitalist machine, or 'the ideal collective capitalist', and in the period since the early 1980s it has gone to great lengths to globalize labour markets and render them precarious.[9] The result of this development has been disastrous in many places, as evidenced by a fall in real wages and a reduction in purchasing power. Loren Goldner calls the period from 1975 to 2008 'the long crash landing' – because social reproduction was increasingly cut back.[10]

Because the state has spearheaded the dismantling of welfare – whether of pensions, unemployment benefits or food subsidies, as happened in Egypt in 2011 – at the same time as it launched large-scale privatization projects, it is precisely the state that is under fire when people take to the streets. Class struggle today is, first and foremost, a refusal of the state and of the way it manages society's shrinking wealth. If the state has always been the henchman of the capitalist class, obviously by securing private property rights, but also by creating a framework for factory labour through factory laws that date back to the early nineteenth century, today it appears in many places as being one with capital. As Jean-Luc Nancy puts it, politics has been 'dissolved in business and the stock exchange'.[11] Attacking the state today is thus an attack on the economy, too. Any attack on the capitalist class is now channelled through the state, which is the object of critique, but also – somehow – the mediator of the anger that's being expressed.

The Grand Débat (Great Debate) launched by Macron in 2019 was one of the more bizarre attempts to balance between these two positions. The state was appealing to citizens for a common good that had long since disappeared, even as the very reason why these citizens took to the streets in the first place was the state itself.

10

Dissolution

The emerging refusal of late capitalism's miserable world is not only short-circuited by the late capitalist fascists, who identify the structural contradictions of a crisis-ridden economy with 'the foreigner' – whether this takes the form of migrants, young people who do not want to reproduce cisgender and heteronormative patterns of life, or theories about the structural violence of modern society like critical race theory. The new opposition is also countered by the extreme centre, that is, by all the old parties that still exist, as well as by the new ones, which are desperately trying to present themselves as something new but are in fact mere hollowed out versions of the old – and increasingly so; Macron's party called Renaissance is a prime example. The political centre refuses to face the fact that the world of Pax Americana no longer makes sense for ever larger parts of the world's population, including more and more people in the West.[1] If it wasn't already clear to most, the brutal bombing of Gaza by the Israeli army in response to Hamas' action on 7 October 2023 has shown what the West's idea of humanism is really about. The human cost of Israeli warfare casts a revealing light on any reference to an international legal order. The scale of the military campaign is overwhelming: the Israel Defense Forces has dropped on Gaza more than 85,000 tonnes of bombs, which is the equivalent of more than four Hiroshima atomic bombs on an area twice the size of Washington DC but home to 2.2 million people. That the Long Peace after 1945/1989 was never particularly peaceful was always clear to most people outside the West, but the contradictions have now become painfully clear.

Millions of people around the world have mobilized, disgusted by the Israeli government's policies and by continued Western support for Israel as a Jewish apartheid state with settlements, with a differentiated legal system, and with more than seventy-five years of low-intensity warfare interrupted by a series of military campaigns – and we should bear in mind that the latest one has reduced Gaza to a pile of rubble and has cost the lives of more than 50,000 people, mostly women and children. The young Moroccan journalist Sania Mahyou has written about the possibility of a 'Palestinian Spring'.[2] And in most places the opposition to genocide is not a movement that supports Hamas. Only a few take to the streets shouting the names of Ismail Haniyeh, Yahya Sinwar or Khaled Marshal. What the protesters and the many students who occupy their universities are rejecting is an Israeli war machine and a United States-led world order that not only allows but actually facilitates genocide. If in 1968 the protesters on the streets of Berlin, Paris and Berkeley chanted 'Ho, Ho, Ho Chi Minh', today there is no identifiable local leader to rely on, in Palestine or anywhere else. As in all current mass protests, the protesters' shout 'from the river to the sea, Palestine will be free' is one of refusal rather than affirmation. It expresses a demand for the dismantling of the Israeli settler state much more than a vision of some new Palestinian state, or a one-state solution – which still recurs here and there, amid the many slogans and calls. Post-war anti-imperialism was rooted in national revolutionary states; today anti-imperialism is not an existing perspective, but merely a historical reference in line with all the other positions that have disappeared and have not been replaced by new ones. There are no heroes in distant lands with which to identify and find inspiration. For better or worse, it is the complicity of their own countries that makes the students occupy campuses and pushes the protesters to take to the streets.

The crisis of capital is thus matched by the destruction of the revolutionary imaginaries of the past two centuries. As the Jamaican American anthropologist David Scott put it, we are in a 'historical conjuncture in which the triumphalist narratives of national liberation, anti-imperialism, and socialism have become exhausted'.[3] The notion of the post-colonial national revolutionary state as redemption and as a home – 'the world-historical answer to the moral–political question about the harms of colonialism' – no longer exists.[4] Scott writes about Jamaica and Latin America, but of course the picture is the same in North Africa and the Middle East. The Arab Spring was crushed by state terror or civil war, as in Syria; and even Tunisia, where the revolutionary process went on the longest, is once again a lumpen dictatorship. It all turned out to be 'half a revolution or no revolution', as Asef Bayat put it in his analysis of the 2010–11 revolts in Egypt and Tunisia.[5] Scott goes so far as to write that 'anti-colonial utopias' have been transformed into 'post-colonial nightmares'.[6] Palestine is the all-too-sad proof of this situation. In a Middle Eastern context, Hamas testifies to a development in which the dream of Arab autonomy as a challenge to Western imperialism fell apart and was replaced by the anti-systemic perspective of Islamist movements. This perspective is not national liberation, as Hamas itself imagines it to be, but the abolition of racial capitalism. It is the revolutionary perspective of the Gaza demonstrations, be they in Tangier, Cairo, Amman, or even Copenhagen or London: not a fight for a Palestinian state but a radical critique of the world order that enables genocide.

All this takes place as a refusal of the local and global order. As Haidar Eid has described, all the established parts of the Palestinian resistance – not only the reactionary factions such as Hamas and Fatah but also the Popular Front for the

Liberation of Palestine and the Democratic Front for the Liberation of Palestine – appear illegitimate and corrupt to most young people.[7] As almost everywhere else, none of the established actors, right or left, can offer anything but false solutions and more misery. That's why so many young people refuse. As Eid puts it, Palestinians are increasingly 'dis-participating' and keeping their distance from the established parties and organizations. 'To dis-participate is to put the legitimacy of the existing order at stake ... It means rejecting the existing system and its political and ideological bias and revealing and opposing its exploitative, distortive, and authoritarian features.'[8]

11

Refusal of the Refusal

Many commentators describe the present conjuncture as a polycrisis. We are still living in the aftermaths of the financial crisis of 2008, which developed into a longer economic crisis with inflation and slow growth – what economists now refer to as secular stagnation; in fact Marxists have long argued that we are going through a phase of shrinking productivity that has already extended for five decades. We have on our hands the climate crisis, which seemingly matters to politicians only when they attend Conference of the Parties (COP) meetings. We then experienced the Covid-19 pandemic, which suddenly changed everything for almost everyone. The reaction to all these crises – 'the epochal crisis', as Nancy Fraser summarizes them – has been to accelerate them, much to the astonishment of the last surviving global liberal forces of the 1990s.[1] Both Bill Clinton's and Hardt and Negri's visions of a post-national or cosmopolitan empire characterized by US hegemony or by the multitude's never-failing capacity to invent are in ruins. The only game that remains is that of gaining access to state offices in order to advance one's own particular faction of the local capitalist class, as when Trump favoured the arms, energy and finance sector of American capital after his election victory in 2016 or when he erected a veritable racket with Musk and the authoritarian tech broligarchy after his second election in 2024. In countries such as the United States it is hard to see the state as anything but special groups of armed men, as Friedrich Engels put it.[2] Little is left of the idea of the state as a common good or instrument of welfare for the masses. In many places it is difficult to distinguish between politicians and organized crime. Everyone is desperately fighting to amass a giant a pool of money while waiting for the next big economic crisis to hit or for the geopolitical dispute to expand from proxy and trade wars to actual military conflicts.

This 'objective dissolution' – the structural violence of racial capitalism, where capitalist development is in equal measure underdevelopment and exclusion – can no doubt continue for a very long time. But it can also be challenged and given a different direction. It can be qualified and turned into a completely different kind of dissolution, which would spell the end of the capitalist destruction that the world suffers – and indeed has suffered for far too long. In three small books, the Invisible Committee has described the scope of the transformation that the many mass protests are tasked with. It is not just a question of small or large changes to society as it has existed since the Second World War. As the Committee explains, what is at stake is an anthropological transformation: an awful lot has to change, both at a societal and at a personal level. For Westerners, this kind of work involves a massive dose of self-criticism. 'Inasmuch as "being someone" always comes down finally to the recognition of, the allegiance to, some institution, inasmuch as succeeding involves conforming to the reflection that you're shown in the hall of mirrors of the social game, the institution has a grip on everyone through the Self.'[3] To paraphrase James Boggs, an African American revolutionary and factory worker, inside every Westerner is accumulated all the racial–colonial violence that has made possible the technological advances that have created our current welfare and police state.[4] To dismantle this violence that we all harbour, together with all the racist class alliances that have sustained and expanded it throughout history, will be as extensive as the fight against the capitalist economy. Hakim Bey once described this task as the greater and lesser jihad, the greater being the desubjectivization, the radical transformation of one's self, and the lesser the suppression of money in all its forms and of the economy as a specialized field of human activity – in short, the end of waged labour.[5]

In his descriptions of the Iranian Revolution published as a series of newspaper articles in the Italian daily *Corriere della Sera*, Michel Foucault noted how an uprising can be an inner journey.[6] 'It is risking no longer being oneself.'[7] This is why Foucault chose to label the events in Iran an uprising and not a revolution. If a 'revolution' is a socio-material transformation in which the ownership of the means of production changes hands from one class to another, what happened on the streets of Tehran, Qom and elsewhere was different. For Foucault, what mattered was how the million-strong demonstrators rejected the regime's way of identifying them:

> In rising up, the Iranians said to themselves – and this perhaps is the soul of the uprising: Of course, we have to change this regime and get rid of this man [the Shah] . . . we have to change the whole country, the political organization, the economic system, the foreign policy. But, above all, we have to change ourselves. Our way of being, our relationship with others, with things, with eternity, with God, etc., must be completely changed, and there will only be a true revolution if this radical change in our experience takes place.[8]

In retrospect, it is clear that what happened in Iran in 1979 was also a revolution that ended with Khomeini's taking power and establishing a repressive theocracy alongside the reactionary Islamist movement he led. But before Khomeini's counter-offensive destroyed the workers' councils, Foucault saw something else, which he described as a subjective uprising. It was not class struggle and political emancipation in the tradition of the French and Russian revolutions that the philosopher glimpsed during his visits to Iran. He described the revolutionary events as a displacement of the identity of the protesters, a transformation, a disruption that affected people 'to the point of renouncing their own individuality, their own subject position'.[9]

We see something similar taking place in the new protests. These are protests, occupations, demonstrations and encampments that do not take place according to a pre-established political programme, but instead reject the political order in its totality. All political self-evidence is abandoned. Away with the old regime, as the Tunisian protesters shouted. Away with all the oppressive institutions, big and small. Even when the mass protests take place around an identity, as in the rejection of anti-black violence in the George Floyd revolt, there is a displacement wherein all the different identities dissolve and become what we can call, with Agamben, the 'whatever singularity'.[10] The incineration of the third police precinct in Minneapolis and of the city hall in Reno, Nevada, and all the looting that took place in countless cities – none of these expressed demands for a less racist police or for body cams on officers. What happened in the streets was a radical refusal of state institutions and identities of late capitalist society; a transgression of the representations and self-representations that are used to separate us from one another and from ourselves. The exaggerated attempt to conflate protests like the George Floyd revolt with demands and make them a matter of identities, make them *someone's*, testifies to the fundamental insecurity of the state. The images of Nancy Pelosi and other Democratic members of Congress kneeling with kente scarves in the Capitol building, and the images of plainclothes officers removing protesters from Lafayette Square so Trump could pose with a Bible in hand in front of St John's Episcopal Church in Washington DC speak volumes. The state is also subject to spectacular conditions and must constantly facilitate capital's increasingly exaggerated destruction and production of identity. When suddenly there is a rupture and many refuse to participate in this process, the state begins to stagger, sends more police on the streets, and stages mind-numbing photo ops to contain the refusal within the already established structure.

Adrian Wohlleben has described what happens when a protest transcends itself.[11] A protest crosses a threshold and achieves what Wohlleben describes as 'strategic autonomy'. In other words the protest gains its own agency, lets go of its starting point and becomes about much more than what the initial mobilization was about. Examples of such processes are legion in the new protest cycle: Macron quickly abandoned his petrol tax, but that in no way made the Yellow Vests go home. And in Hong Kong protesters continued their actions after Carrie Lam postponed the extradition bill they were protesting against. In both cases, the protests metamorphosized and became much larger. It therefore made no difference when the state rolled back its taxes or its laws. The protests continued unabated. It was as if the protesters realized that they could get away with doing things they were otherwise prevented from doing. It became possible to share the world in a completely different way, beyond any idea of crime and property rights. As Wohlleben writes: 'Wherever the virtual coordinates of the antagonism shift, no backtracking is possible.'[12] The French sociologist Romain Huët describes this as 'the vertigo of riots', in which there is an 'ontological opening' and the fixed structures of the world become unstable or begin to crack.[13]

As in the case of the Arab Spring, the Yellow Vests or Argentina 2001, only *after* the protests have taken place is it possible to reconstruct a causality, even if the latter will always be slightly skewed or reductive. Labour market reforms, fuel taxes or austerity policies are never the real causes; or they might be, once enough people take to the streets and refuse, allowing for a condensation to occur that then explodes. 'None of these dissimilar memories can be understood as a cause, for they only act as such once they have entered under the dynamic that actualizes them.'[14] There is a shift, causal connections dissolve, and another space opens up in the protest. This is what Foucault sensed in Tehran in 1979 and what Walter Benjamin and Furio Jesi both noted in their analyses of the German Revolution of 1919.[15] Homogeneous, chronological and abstract time is suspended in mass protests when people refuse.

In a series of texts drawing upon Frantz Fanon, Cecil Taylor and Hortense Spillers, Fred Moten describes a paradoxical process of self-abolition in which the slave rejects the denial of freedom.[16] The black slave is the paradigmatic example of an individual denied subjectivity. With a reference to anti-colonialism and Black feminism, Moten conceives of the struggle against the enslavement of people from Africa as a refusal of this refusal. When the Black slave escapes – Moten often mentions Harriet Jacobs – that is not an act of liberation through which she aspires to become a subject and a citizen and thereby achieve political recognition and legal status. It is a refusal of the entire political, economic, legal and scientific order that produces her as an object – the order that produces Blackness as radical exclusion, the impossibility of being a subject with self-awareness and agency. Black fugitivity is an act of resistance that avoids recognizing the structure, an act in which the Black person is always already flesh, a body without legal status that cannot enter into the struggle for political recognition.

Moten's analysis is a contribution to the understanding of refusal as a radical shift in which the need to be a subject is loosened and problematized – as when Fannie Lou Hamer radically questions what it means to be a US citizen and attempts to run for the Democratic nomination in Mississippi in 1964, but the following year participates in demonstrations against the Vietnam War.[17]

Hamer challenges anti-Black racism, according to which she cannot participate in political discussions, but she also rejects the entire structure on which it rests, and thus the United States as a racial–capitalist war state. In so doing, she questions the notion of freedom itself and asks: what if this freedom is actually a mechanical part in the very structure that constantly destroys all the worlds that could exist but never see the light of day? What if the notion of freedom and the idea of humanity it defines are actually a prison? In doing so, according to Moten, she rejects the freedom she has been denied. She refuses to exist as a subject. She escapes the bounded singular subject and becomes something else.

This radical refusal of misery and oppression is reflected in the many demonstrations, riots, revolts and occupations of the new protest cycle. Everywhere people take to the streets and refuse. They do so from different vantage points, of course – there is a difference between a white cisgender male body in the United Kingdom and a Black trans body in the United States or a brown lesbian body in Mexico; but on the streets they are united in refusing this world and its models of sovereignty.

REFUSAL OF THE REFUSAL

It is difficult to avoid being caught in a deadly dialectic with the state, where it remains the horizon of all your gestures, whether these take the form of compromises or militant actions. With Jacobs and Hamer, we can say that refusal must be a refusal *of* refusal. The state always 'offers' something other than what is being fought for, and it is not the state that the new disobedient subjects are interested in. It is wrong that we cannot exist without it and its subject forms. It is no longer a question of becoming a revolutionary, even less a leftist or an activist. The new protests are no longer about getting recognized by institutions or securing a share in running the whole thing. Power is something to be avoided, not something to aspire to or fight for. The refusal of refusal extends the struggle beyond reformist or terrorist dead ends and suspends the heated struggle for identity. We take to the streets for Palestine and for Black lives, but something other than the oppressed and oppressive representations emerges when we find one another there, together. New forms of life that cannot be recognized by late capitalism's diverse modes of control and necropolitics.

What is really new in the mass protests that continue to take place is that no one believes they have discovered, in this new bubbling over of forces and ideas, the birth of a new party, as has always been the case throughout the twentieth century – not even in events like May 1968 or 1977 in Bologna, where the old parties were being violently refused. This is precisely what we must affirm today: the absence of a party, with all that this implies. True, many people still try to recall, and thus revive, old organizational and party theories.[18] But the movement of refusal is the negation of this attempt. It is what we hear in the constant cry that *all the leaders must go*. The refusal is so massive that it points towards a radical transformation, the end of the world as we know it. There should be nothing left when the protests are over – not even a small annex or some extension from which a new power can emerge and impose its laws. As Marcello Tarì puts it, '[t]here is no *necessity* of power, only a decadent tradition that continues to postulate it'.[19] This is the perspective of the movement of refusal: the concrete dismantling of all laws and all the forms of power that maintain them. A refusal of refusal, or an annihilation of nothing. This is the task of the Refusalist International.

Notes

Epigraph Credits

1 Lines from *Human Strike Has Already Begun and Other Writings*, by Claire Fontaine. Published in 2013 by Mute. Reprinted with permission.
2 Line from 'New Black Music', in the collection Black Music, by Amiri Baraka/LeRoi Jones (William Morrow, 1967). Reissued in 2010 by Akashic Books. Reprinted with permission.

Notes to Chapter 1

1 Herbert Marcuse, *One-Dimensional Man: Studies in the Ideology of Advanced Industrial Society* [1964] (London: Routledge, 2006), 257.
2 Marcuse had already written about 'the great refusal' in 1955: 'The Great Refusal is the protest against unnecessary repression, the struggle for the ultimate

form of freedom – "to live without anxiety".' Herbert Marcuse, *Eros and Civilization* [1955] (Boston, MA: Beacon Press, 1974), 149–50. Marcuse refers here to Alfred North Whitehead's use of the concept of refusal, which describes the determination not to succumb to the facticity of things as they are. 'The truth that some proposition respecting an actual occasion is untrue may express the vital truth as to the aesthetic achievement. It expresses the "great refusal" which is its primary characteristic.' Alfred North Whitehead, *Science and the Modern World* (New York: Macmillan, 1926), 228 (as cited in *Eros and Civilization*, 149).

3 Marcuse, *One-Dimensional Man*, xliv.
4 Ibid., 259.
5 Ibid.
6 Herbert Marcuse, *An Essay on Liberation* (Boston, MA: Beacon Press, 1969), 10.
7 Marcuse, *One-Dimensional Man*, 257.
8 Ibid., 260.
9 Ibid.
10 Ibid., 260–1.
11 Ibid., 260.
12 Herbert Marcuse, 'Revolutionary Subject and Self-Government', *Praxis* 5.2 (1969), 328.

Notes to Chapter 2

1 Christian Stirling Haig, Katherine Schmidt and Samuel Brannen, 'The Age of Mass Protests: Understanding an Escalating Global Trend', *CSIS: Center for Strategic &*

International Studies, 2 March 2020, https://www.csis.org/analysis/age-mass-protests-understanding-escalating-global-trend.
2 Giorgio Cesarano, *Manuale di sopravvivenza* [1974] (Turin: Bollati Boringhieri, 2000), 66.
3 Dilip Gaonkar, 'Demos Noir: Riot after Riot', in Natasha Ginwala, Gal Kirn and Niloufar Tajeri, eds, *Nights of the Dispossessed: Riots Unbound* (New York: Columbia University Press, 2021), 31.
4 Judith Butler, *Notes toward a Performative Theory of Assembly* (Cambridge, MA: Harvard University Press, 2015), 139.
5 Over more than fifteen years, Alain Bertho has meticulously collected data on mass protests on his homepage 'Emeutes: Base documentaire', https://berthoalain.com/documents. See also Carnegie Endowment for International Peace: 'Global Protest Tracker', https://carnegieendowment.org/features/global-protest-tracker?lang=en.
6 Michalis Lianos, 'Une politique expérientielle: Les gilets jaunes en tant que "peuple"', *Lundi Matin*, 170, 19 December 2018, https://lundi.am/Une-politique-experientielle-Les-gilets-jaunes-en-tant-que-peuple.
7 Tristan Leoni, *Sur les gilets jaunes: Du trop de réalité* (Geneva: Entremonde, 2023), 24.
8 On this point, see Serge Quadruppani, *Le monde des grands projets et ses ennemis: Voyage au cœur des nouvelles pratiques révolutionnaires* (Paris: La Découverte, 2018).
9 Donatella Di Cesare, *The Time of Revolt* [2020] (Cambridge: Polity, 2022).

10 Rodrigo Karmy, *The Future Is Inherited: Fragments of a Chile in Revolt* [2019] (Berlin: Errant Bodies, 2022), 11.
11 Ibid., 52.

Notes to Chapter 3

1 Judith Butler, for example, writes: 'Of course we are right to distinguish among kinds of protest, differentiating antimilitarization movements from precarity movements. . . . At the same time, precarity seems to run through a variety of such movements, whether it is the precarity of those killed in war, those who lack basic infrastructure, those who are exposed to disproportionate violence on the streets, or those who seek to gain an education at the cost of unpayable debt.' Butler, *Notes toward a Performative Theory of Assembly*, 17–18.
2 Michael Hardt and Antonio Negri, *Declaration* (New York: Argo Navis, 2013), 4.
3 'Les peuples veulent la chute des régimes', *Lundi Matin* 169, 14 December 2018, https://lundi.am/Les-peuples-veulent-la-chute-des-regimes.
4 For analyses of the square occupation tactic, see the texts collected by Michael Hardt in a mini-dossier in M. Hardt, 'Falsify the Currency!', *South Atlantic Quarterly* 111.3 (2012), 564–615.
5 For a good description of the frontliner tactic and its use, see 'Welcome to the Frontlines: Beyond Violence and Nonviolence', Chuang blog, 8 June 2020, https://chuangcn.org/2020/06/frontlines.

6   See n. 5 in the previous chapter.
7   Di Cesare, *The Time of Revolt*, 1.
8   Shemon Salam and Arturo Castillon, 'The Return of John Brown: White Race-Traitors in the 2020 Uprising', Ill Will, 4 September 2020, https://illwill.com/the-return-of-john-brown-white-race-traitors-in-the-2020-uprising.
9   Marcello Tarì, *There Is No Unhappy Revolution: The Communism of Destitution* [2017] (New York: Common Notions, 2021).
10 Hamid Dabashi, *The Arab Spring: The End of Postcolonialism* (London: Zed Books, 2012), 3.
11 Colectivo Situaciones, *19 & 20: Notes for a New Social Protagonism* [2002] (Wivenhoe, Colchester: Minor Compositions, 2011), 52.
12 Ibid., 37.
13 Ibid., 26.

Notes to Chapter 4

1   Maurice Blanchot, 'Refusal' [1958], in Maurice Blanchot, *Political Writings, 1953–1993* (New York: Fordham University Press, 2010), 7. For a presentation of Blanchot's short text and its context, see Mikkel Bolt Rasmussen, 'An Affirmation That Is Entirely Other', *South Atlantic Quarterly* 122.1 (2023), 19–31.
2   Blanchot, 'Refusal', 7.
3   Ibid.
4   Ibid.
5   Giorgio Agamben, *The Coming Community* [1990] (Minneapolis: University of Minnesota Press, 1993), 65.

6 For a discussion of the difference between the historical party and all the formally existing parties, that is, political organizations with programmes, central committees and members, see Amadeo Bordiga, 'Considerations on the Party's Organic Activity When the General Situation Is Historically Unfavorable', 1965, https://www.marxists.org/archive/bordiga/works/1965/consider.htm.
7 Fred Moten, *Consent Not to Be a Single Being: Stolen Life* (Durham, NC: Duke University Press, 2018), 189.
8 Ibid., 188.

Notes to Chapter 5

1 For a good analysis of the course of events in Tunisia and Egypt, where revolutionary uprisings were derailed by elections, manipulations and military coups – quickly in Egypt, more slowly in Tunisia – see Gilbert Achcar, *Morbid Symptoms: Relapse in the Arab Spring* (London: Saqi Books Press, 2016).
2 Jean-Claude Milner, *La destitution du peuple* (Paris: Verdier, 2022).
3 Ibid., 39.
4 Ibid., 40.

Notes to Chapter 6

1 Mark Fisher, *Capitalist Realism: Is There No Alternative?* (Winchester: Zero Books, 2009). Jacques Rancière uses the phrase 'consensual administration' in his analysis of the depoliticization that has taken place throughout

the 1990s and 2000s: Jacques Rancière, *Chronicles of Consensual Times* [2005] (London: Bloomsbury, 2010).
2 George W. Bush, as quoted by Slavoj Žižek, 'Resistance Is Surrender', in *London Review of Books* 29.22 (2007), 7.
3 Vincent Bevins, *If We Burn: The Mass Protest Decade and The Missing Revolution* (London: Wildfire, 2023).
4 Kurt Andersen, 'Person of the Year: The Protester', *Time*, 14 December 2011, https://content.time.com/time/specials/packages/article/0,28804,2101745_2102132,00.html. Robin Wright, 'The Story of 2019: Protests in Every Corner of the Globe', *The New Yorker*, 30 December 2019, https://www.newyorker.com/news/our-columnists/the-story-of-2019-protests-in-every-corner-of-the-globe.
5 'The Power of Protest', *The Economist*, 13 June 2020, 7.
6 Jim Reid et al., 'The Age of Disorder', 2020, Deutsche Bank, 9 September, https://www.dbresearch.com/PROD/RPS_EN-PROD/PROD0000000000511857/The_Age_of_Disorder_%E2%80%93_the_new_era_for_economics%2C_p.xhtml.
7 Gianfranco Sanguinetti (Censor), *The Real Report on the Last Chance to Save Capitalism in Italy* [1975] (Fort Bragg, NC: Flatland Books, 1997).
8 SIPRI (Stockholm International Peace Research Institute), 'Trends in World Military Expenditure', *SIPRI Fact Sheet*, 22 April 2024, https://reliefweb.int/report/world/sipri-fact-sheet-april-2024-trends-world-military-expenditure-2023-encasv.
9 See *Conspiracist Manifesto* [2022] (Los Angeles: Semiotex(e), 2023).

10 Of course, this does not mean that there is a causal relationship between economic misery and more radical protests and uprisings. As a whole generation of Marxists realized in the interwar period, 'the political' does not necessarily go 'left' when 'the economy' does. In this sense, protests are not a 'sociological' phenomenon that can be reduced to causality. Identifying the actual causes of an uprising is not possible. Rather, as Walter Benjamin explains, uprisings are a short circuit between past and present in which historical continuity is suspended: Walter Benjamin, 'On the Concept of History' [1940], in Walter Benjamin, *Selected Writings*, vol. 4: *1938–1940* (Cambridge, MA: Harvard University Press, 2003), 389–400.

11 Bordiga, 'Considerations on the Party's Organic Activity'.

Notes to Chapter 7

1 T. J. Clark, 'Capitalism without Images', in Kevin Coleman and Daniel James, eds, *Capitalism and the Camera: Essays on Photography and Extraction* (London: Verso, 2021), 120–41.

2 Ibid., 126.

3 'Le déclin et la chute de l'économie spectaculaire-marchande', *Internationale situationniste* 10 (1966), 3–11; translated into English as 'The Decline and Fall of the Spectacle-Commodity Economy', https://theanarchistlibrary.org/library/situationist-international-the-decline-and-fall-of-the-spectacle-commodity-economy.

4 Clark, 'Capitalism without Images', 126.

5 Ibid., 132.
6 Ibid., 140.
7 Ibid., 125.

Notes to Chapter 8

1 'A History of Separation', *Endnotes* 4 (2015), 70–192. For a good presentation of Théorie Communiste's periodisation, see 'Sur la restructuration et le nouveau cycle de luttes', *Théorie communiste* 16 (2000), 28–63.
2 Karl Marx and Friedrich Engels, *Manifesto of the Communist Party* [1848], in Karl Marx and Friedrich Engels, *Collected Works*, vol. 6: *Marx and Engels, 1845–48* (London: Lawrence & Wishart, 1976), 477–519.
3 'In April 1848, Engels, then in Barmen, was translating the *Manifesto* into English, but he managed to translate only half of it, and the first English translation, made by Helen Macfarlane, was not published until two years later, between June and November 1850, in the Chartist journal *The Red Republican*. Its editor, Julian Harney, named the authors for the first time in the introduction to this publication. All earlier and many subsequent editions of the *Manifesto* were anonymous.' Quoted from the Preface to the 1888 English edition of the *Manifesto*, https://www.marxists.org/archive/marx/works/download/pdf/Manifesto.pdf.
4 'Prolétariat et capital: Une trop brève idylle?', *Théorie communiste* 19 (2004), 5–60.
5 Marx and Engels, *Manifesto of the Communist Party*, 496.
6 Ibid., 496.

7 Later on Marx revised the teleological view of history according to which the social revolution of the industrial proletariat was destined to complete the political revolution of the bourgeoisie. One of the problems with this view was that it tended to make the development of the highly developed centre the model for all other places, as if Manchester and, later, Detroit were the matrix for St Petersburg, Mumbai or Cairo. In retrospect, it is striking how far outside the centre of capital accumulation the revolutions of the twentieth century actually happened: Russia, Mexico, China, Cuba, Algeria, Vietnam, Iran, etc.

8 Michael Denning, 'Neither Capitalist, Nor American: The Democracy as Social Movement', in Michael Denning, *Culture in the Age of Three Worlds* (London: Verso, 2004), 209–26; Geoff Eley, *Forging Democracy: The History of the Left in Europe, 1850–2000* (Oxford: Oxford University Press, 2002); Göran Therborn, 'The Rule of Capital and the Rise of Democracy', *New Left Review* 103 (1977), 3–41.

9 Aimé Césaire, 'Letter to Maurize Thorez' [1956], *Social Text* 28.2 (2010), 145–52.

10 Silvia Federici, *Revolution at Point Zero: Housework, Reproduction, and Feminist Struggle* (Oakland, CA: PM Press, 2012), 7.

Notes to Chapter 9

1 Mario Tronti, 'Towards a Critique of Political Democracy' [2007], *Cosmos and History* 5.1 (2009), 68–75.

2 Ibid., 73.
3 For a fine contemporary description, see Daniel Cohn-Bendit and Gabriel Cohn-Bendit, *Obsolete Communism: The Left-Wing Alternative* [1968] (New York: McGraw-Hill Book Company, 1968).
4 Guy Debord, *The Society of the Spectacle* [1967] (New York: Zone Books, 1995), 70–1.
5 Hall's articles from the late 1970s to the mid-1980s on Thatcher's authoritarian populism are both a good and and a bad example of this. See Stuart Hall, *The Hard Road to Renewal: Thatcherism and the Crisis of the Left* (London: Verso, 1988).
6 Carla Lonzi, *Sputiamo su Hegel: La donna clitoridea e la donna vaginale e altri scritti* (Milan: Rivolta femminile, 1974).
7 See books such as François Danel, ed., *Rupture dans la théorie de la révolution* (Paris: Senonevero, 2003); Roland Simon, *Fondements critiques d'une théorie de la révolution: Au-delà de l'affirmation du prolétariat* (Paris: Senonevero, 2001); and the previously cited 'A History of Separation'.
8 Joshua Clover, *Riot: Strike: Riot: The New Era of Uprisings* (London: Verso, 2016).
9 Paul Mattick, 'On the Concept of State-Monopoly Capitalism', 1977. Paul Mattick Archive, https://www.marxists.org/archive/mattick-paul/1977/inflation/ch04.htm.
10 Loren Goldner, 'The Historical Moment That Produced Us', *Insurgent Notes* 1 (2010), http://insurgentnotes.com/2010/06/historical_moment.
11 Jean-Luc Nancy, 'Pour répondre à l'appel de Julien Coupat

et Eric Hazan', *Libération*, 11 February 2016, https://www.liberation.fr/debats/2016/02/11/pour-repondre-a-l-appel-de-julien-coupat-et-d-eric-hazan_1432682.

Notes to Chapter 10

1 When the situation comes to a head, the new fascists emerge and act as power conductors with a displaced critique of the 'global elites' and the 'system'. See Mikkel Bolt Rasmussen, *Late Capitalist Fascism* (Cambridge: Polity, 2022).
2 Sania Mahyou, 'Can Israel's War on Gaza Trigger a "Palestinian Spring" in the Arab World?', *The New Arab*, 10 April 2024, https://www.newarab.com/opinion/can-gaza-trigger-palestinian-spring-arab-world.
3 David Scott, 'The Tragic Vision in Postcolonial Time', *PMLA* 129.4 (2014), 799.
4 Ibid., 806.
5 Asef Bayat, *Revolution without Revolutionaries: Making Sense of the Arab Spring* (Stanford, CA: Stanford University Press, 2017), 154.
6 David Scott, *Conscripts of Modernity: The Tragedy of Colonial Enlightenment* (Durham, NC: Duke University Press, 2004), 2.
7 Haidar Eid, 'The Urgent Need to Revitalize the Palestinian Left', Mondoweiss, 25 January, 2021, https://mondoweiss.net/2021/01/the-urgent-need-to-revitalize-the-palestinian-left.
8 Haidar Eid, 'Dis-Participation as a Palestinian Strategy?', Al-Shabaka: The Palestinian Policy Network,

9 December 2013, https://al-shabaka.org/commentaries/dis-participation-as-a-palestinian-strategy.

Notes to Chapter 11

1 Nancy Fraser, 'Climates of Capital', *New Left Review* 127 (2021), 95.
2 Friedrich Engels, *The Origin of the Family, Private Property and the State* [1884], in Karl Marx and Friedrich Engels, *Collected Works*, vol. 26: *Engels, 1882–1889* (London: Lawrence and Wishart, 1990), 270.
3 The Invisible Committee, *Now* (Los Angeles, CA: Semiotext(e), 2017), 74–5.
4 James Boggs, *American Revolution: Pages from a Negro Worker's Notebook* [1963] (New York: Monthly Review Press, 2009), 45. Boggs is of course writing specifically about the United States.
5 Hakim Bey, *Millenium* (New York: Autonomedia, 1996), 20–1.
6 Two good analyses of Foucault's articles from Iran are Behrooz Ghamari-Tabrizi, *Foucault in Iran: Islamic Revolution after the Enlightenment* (Minneapolis: University of Minnesota Press, 2016) and Alain Brossat and Alain Naze, *Interroger l'actualité, avec Michel Foucault: Tehran 1978 / Paris 2015* (Paris: Eterotopia, 2018).
7 Michel Foucault, 'Political Spirituality as the Will for Alterity: An Interview with the *Nouvel Observateur*', *Critical Inquiry* 47 (2020), 129. The interview was done in 1979 but published posthumously, first in French

in 2018 in a partial version, then in full in English in 2020.
8. Michel Foucault, 'Iran: The Spirit of a World without Spirit' [1978], in Janet Afary and Kevin B. Anderson, *Foucault and the Iranian Revolution: Gender and the Seduction of Islamism* (Chicago, IL: Chicago University Press, 2005), 255.
9. Foucault, 'Political Spirituality as the Will for Alterity', 124.
10. Agamben, *The Coming Community*, 113–16.
11. Adrian Wohlleben, 'Autonomy in Conflict', Ill Will, 29 June 2023, https://illwill.com/autonomy-in-conflict.
12. Ibid.
13. Romain Huët, *Le vertige de l'émeute: De la Zad aux Gilets jaunes* (Paris: PUF: 2019), 10–11.
14. Colectivo Situaciones, *19 & 20*, 69.
15. Walter Benjamin, 'Critique of Violence' [1921], in Walter Benjamin, *Selected Writings*, vol. 1: *1913–1926* (Cambridge, MA: Harvard University Press, 1996), 236–52; Furio Jesi, *Spartakus: The Symbology of Revolt* [1969] (London: Seagull, 2014).
16. Among the many texts collected in Fred Moten, *Consent Not to Be a Single Being* (Durham, NC: Duke University Press, 2017–2018), see especially 'Chromatic Saturation', from *Stolen Life*, 140–246.
17. Fred Moten in conversation with Saidiya Hartman, 'To Refuse That Which Has Been Refused to You', *Chimurenga*, 19 October 2018, https://chimurengachronic.co.za/to-refuse-that-which-has-been-refused-to-you-2.

18 Vincent Bevins, for example, ends his otherwise excellent journalistic presentation of protests in Brazil, Indonesia, Ukraine, Hong Kong and Egypt by concluding that the revolution never happened because the protesters were not organized as in the good old days, in other words as a political party: Bevins, *If We Burn*, 281–6. With this he misses the most important aspect of the new protests and paradoxically overlooks the political experimentation and self-theorization that is taking place.
19 Marcello Tarì, 'Il partito di Kafka', *Pólemos* 1 (2020), 104.